Data Structures Using C++

B GEETHA KATTI - B.E, M.E
Bangalore

INDIA • SINGAPORE • MALAYSIA

Dedicated to my father

KATTI

and my mother

GOURAMMA

Preface

Data structures form the backbone of efficient programming and software development. A deep understanding of data organization, manipulation, and retrieval is crucial for writing optimized and scalable code. This book, *Data Structures Using C++*, is designed to provide a comprehensive introduction to fundamental and advanced data structures, equipping readers with the knowledge and skills needed to solve computational problems effectively.

The primary objective of this book is to present data structures in a clear and structured manner, with a strong emphasis on practical implementation using C++. Each chapter introduces a specific data structure, explains its theoretical foundations, and provides step-by-step examples to demonstrate its real-world applications.

This book is intended for undergraduate students, self-learners, and professionals who want to strengthen their grasp of data structures using C++. It assumes a basic familiarity with C++ programming and gradually builds upon that foundation. With numerous hands-on exercises, conceptual explanations, and practical coding examples, readers will develop a solid understanding of data structures and their role in efficient algorithm design.

I hope this book serves as a valuable resource in your journey toward mastering data structures. Happy coding!

Email your suggestions to katti.geetha@gmail.com

– B Geetha Katti

Acknowledgements

Writing this book, *Data Structures Using C++*, has been a rewarding journey, and I am deeply grateful to everyone who contributed to its completion.

First and foremost, I extend my heartfelt gratitude to my father **Basappa Rathnakatti** and my mother **Gouramma**, whose guidance and expertise have been invaluable in shaping the content of this book. Their insights and constructive feedback have helped refine complex concepts into clear and accessible explanations.

A special appreciation goes to my sisters **Girija B** and **Latha B** and my brothers **Suresh S Chalageri** and **Bharatesha Matturu** for their unwavering support and encouragement throughout this endeavor. Their patience and belief in my work have been instrumental in bringing this book to life.

I would also like to thank my sons **Chetan S** and **Atharv M.**

Lastly, I would also like to thank my teachers, my students, and readers, whose curiosity and enthusiasm for learning have been a constant source of motivation. Their questions and challenges have inspired me to present data structures in a way that is both engaging and practical.

– **B Geetha Katti**

Synopsis

Contents

CHAPTER - 1

Chapter 1

The Basic C++ Language

Introduction

Programs are a sequence of instructions or statements. These statements form the structure of a C++ program. The structure of a program differs from one programming language to the other. The programmer will make use of datatypes, operators, branching or looping constructs etc., while writing a program. Hence it is very much necessary to know about the basics required to write a program.

Structure

1. The general form of a C++ program
2. Datatypes
3. Operators
4. Branching and looping statements

Objectives:

After reading this chapter, the reader will understand the basic syntax of program in C++, the various datatypes available in C++. The reader can write efficient programs by making use of various operators available in C++. A brief introduction to various branching and looping statements is also given in the book using which the reader can write most effective programs in C++.

1.1   The general form of a C++ program

The general form of C++ program is as shown below:

```
//comment section

Preprocessor directives

Global declaration section

class c_name
```

```
{
    access specifiers:
         datatype1 var1;
         datatype2 var2;
         ...................
         datatypen varn;
         returntype1 func1()
         {
              ......
         }
         ...............
         returntypen funcn()
         {
              ......
         }
};
int main()
{
     Declaration statements
          And
     Executable Statements
}
```

Given below is the detailed explanation of the above general form of a C++ program.

Comment section:

These are the non-executable statements in C++ program. These are two types of comments:

1. Single line comments
2. Multi line comments

Single line comments:

These types of comments start with // and are used when the non-executable statements are of only one line.

Multi line comments:

These types of comments start with /* and end with */ and are used when the comments are of more than a single line.

Section 1: Header file declaration section

1. Header files used in the program are listed here.
2. These are also called as preprocessor directives.

3. Header files provide prototype declaration for different library functions.
4. User header file can also be included.
5. All preprocessor directives are written in this section.
6. They start with symbol # and most commonly used preprocessor directive is **"include"**.

Section 2: Global declaration section

1. Global variables are declared here.
2. Global declaration includes:

   i) Declaring structure
   ii) Declaring class
   iii) Declaring variable

Section 3: Class declaration section

1. Class declaration and all the methods of that class are defined here.
2. The class definition starts with keyword class followed by class name.
3. The class includes the declaration of data members and member functions.

   Data members: The variables declared inside the class are called data members.
   Member functions: The functions defined inside the class are called member functions.

4. The definition of a class ends with ";"(semicolon).

Section 4: Main function section

1. This is entry point for all functions. Each and every method is indirectly called through main function.
2. Class objects are created in main function.
3. Operating system calls main function automatically.
4. The main function includes executable and declaration statements.

Example Program:

```cpp
#include<iostream>
using namespace std;
class sample
{
        int num;
        public:
void read()
        {
                cout<<"enter a number"<<endl;
                cin>>num;
```

```cpp
        }
        void print()
        {
                cout<<"the entered number is"<<num<<endl;
        }
} ;
int main()
{
    Sample obj;
    obj.read();
    obj.print();
    return 0;
}
```

I/O library:

<iostream>

- ➢ The file defines the cin, cout, cerr and clog objects.
- ➢ cin correspond to the standard input stream.
- ➢ cout correspond to the standard output stream.
- ➢ cerr correspond to the standard error stream.
- ➢ clog correspond to the standard error stream.

1.1.1   The standard input stream (cin)

- ➢ The predefined object cin is an object or instance of istream class.
- ➢ The cin object is attached to the standard input device , which is usually the keyboard.
- ➢ The cin is used in conjunction with the stream extraction operator ">>".
- ➢ The extraction operator is overloaded right shift operator "<<".

C++ program to demonstrate the usage of cin or ">>" operator

```cpp
#include<iostream>
using namespace std;
int main()
{
    int a;
    float f;
    string s;

    cout<"Enter an integer value"<<endl;
```

```
    cin>>a;

    cout<<"Enter a floating point value"<<endl;
    cin>>f;

    cout<<"Enter a string"<<endl;
    cin>>s;

    cout<<"The integer value is"<<a<<endl;
    cout<<"The floating point value is"<<f<<endl;
    cout<<"The entered string is""<<s<<endl;

    return 0;
}
```

Output:

```
Enter an integer value
10
Enter a floating point number
10.5
Enter a string
REVA UNIVERSITY
The integer value is 10
The floating point value is 10.5
The entered string is REVA UNIVERSITY
```

Note the following points from the above program:

- ➢ There is no need to specify format specifiers as in case of C language.
- ➢ The C++ compiler also determines the data type of the value entered and selects the appropriate stream extraction operator to extract the value and store it in the given variable.
- ➢ ">>" operator may be used more than once in a single statement.
- ➢ To request / input more than one variable:
- ➢ cin>>a>>f>>s;

1.1.2   The standard output stream (cout)

- ➢ The predefined object cout is an instance or object of "ostream" class.
- ➢ The cout object is said to be "connected to" the standard output device , which is usually the keyboard.

➢ The cout is used in conjunction with stream insertion operator , which is written as << which are "two less than signs or operator"

```
// C++ program to demonstrate the usage of cout or "<<" operator

#include < iostream>
using namespace std;
int main()
{
     string str="Hello Chetan";
     cout<<"value of str is"<<str<<endl;
     return 0;
}
```

Output:

```
value of str is Hello Chetan
```

Note the following points from the above program:

➢ The "<<" operator is overloaded to output data of datatypes like int , float, double, string and pointer values .
➢ The insertion operator "<<" can be used more than once in a single statement.
➢ Example: cout<<str<<a;
➢ endl is used to add a new – line at the end of the line like "\n" in C language.
➢ endl along with "\n" can be used to add a new line.

1.1.3   Preprocessor directives

➢ Preprocessor are programs that processes source code before compilation.
➢ Preprocessor directives begin with a "#" symbol.
➢ The "#" symbol indicates that the statement that starts with "#" , is going to preprocessor program and preprocessor program will execute this statement.
➢ Examples of some preprocessor directives are:

    #include
    #define
    #ifndef

There are **four main types of preprocessor directives**:

1. Macros
2. File inclusion

3. Conditional compilation
4. Other directives

1. Macros:

➢ Macros are a piece of code in a program which is given some name.
➢ Whenever the given name is encountered by the compiler, the compiler replaces the name with the actual piece of code.
➢ The "#define "directive is used to define the macro.

Example program to understand the macro definition:

```cpp
#include<iostream>

#define PI 3.14
using namespace std;
int main()
{
    int radius;
    cout<<"Enter the value of radius"<<endl;

    float area;
    area=radius*radius*PI;

    cout<<"The area of circle is"<<area<<endl;
    return 0;
}
```

Output

```
Enter the value of radius
10
The area of circle is 314
```

Note the following points from the above program:

➢ When the compiler executes the word PI it replaces with 3.14
➢ The word PI is called macro template and the value 3.14 is called macro expansion.
➢ Macro definition do not need a semicolon at the end i.e. there is no semicolon at the end of macro definition.

Macro with arguments:

- ➢ We can pass arguments to macros.
- ➢ Macros defined with arguments works similarly as functions.

```cpp
// C++ program example:
#include<iostream>
#define AREA(L,B) (L*B)

int main()
{
    int len=10,bre=5, area;
    area=AREA(len,bre);

    cout<<"Area of rectangle"<<area<<endl;

    return 0;
}
```

Output

```
Area of rectangle 50
In the above program, the compiler finds AREA(L,B) in the program it replaces it
with the statement (L*B)
```

2. File Inclusion

- ➢ This type of preprocessor directive tells the compiler to include file in the source code program.
- ➢ There are two types of files which can be included by the user in the program.

   Header files or standard files:

   - ➢ These files contain definition of pre – defined functions.
   - ➢ These files should be included for the working of the pre defined functions.
   - ➢ Different functions are declared in different header files.
   - ➢ For example standard I/O functions are in "iostream" file whereas string functions like strlen are include in "string " header file.
     ```
     #include<file_name>
     ```

   User defined files

   - ➢ When a program becomes very large, it is good practice to divide it into smaller files and include whenever needed.

- ➢ These type of files are user defined file.
- ➢ These files can be included as
  #include " filename"

3. Conditional compilation:

- ➢ These directives helps to compile a specific portion of the program or to skip compilation of some part of the program based on some conditions.
- ➢ This can be done with the help of two preprocessing keywords 'ifdef' and 'endif'

  Syntax:
  #ifdef macro_name
  Statement 1;
      Statement 2;
      …..
      ….
      Statement n;
  #endif

- ➢ If the macro with the name "macro_name" is defined then the block of statements following the macro will be executed normally but if it is not defined , the compiler will skip these block of statements.

4. Other directives:

There are two directives which are not commonly used .They are:

- ➢ #undef directive
- ➢ #pragma directive
  #pragma startup
  #pragma exit

5. using directive in C++

using directive allows you to use types defined in a namespace.

Note: This directive is explained in detail later in this book.

1.1.4   Steps to learn a C++ programming language:

Any other regional language   **C++ language**

Alphabets   Character Set   **Eg:**
                                                            Letters: A-Z,a-z
                                                            Numbers: 0-9,
                                                            Special symbols:#,&,*,<,>

Words	Tokens	**Eg:**
		Keywords: int, float, void, struct
		Operators: +,-,*,/
		Constants: 2.2,REVA
		Identifiers: sum, prod
		Special Symbols: +,-,;./,(,),{,},[,]
Sentences	Instructions	**Eg:**
		sum=a+b;
		cout<<sum;
Paragraphs	Program	#include<iostream.h>
		/////////////////
		/////////////////

Token:

A token is a basic unit of any program. One or more characters are grouped in sequence to form meaningful words and these words are called tokens. There tokens in C++ language are classified as shown below:

i)   Keywords
ii)   Identifiers
iii)   Constants
iv)   Operators
v)   Special Symbols

Keywords:

The words which have pre defined meaning in C++ language are called keywords. Since they are reserved for specific purpose in C++ language, these words are called reserved words.

There are 62 keywords in C++ language.

1.2   Basic / Simple / Primitive Datatypes and Variables:

These data types are built-in or predefined data types and can be used directly by the user to declare variables. These are the data types which can be manipulated directly by machine instructions.

The various data types available in C++ language are:

int, float, char, double, bool, void, string

int:

- ➢ An int is a keyword which is used to define integers in C++ language
- ➢ Using int keyword, the programmer can inform the compiler that the
    - a) Data associated with this keyword should be defined as integers.
    - b) Size of the data to be manipulated is determined by the compiler and reserve space in memory to store the data.
    - c) The size of int is machine dependent.
    - d) C++ supports three different sizes of integer datatype:
        - i) short int
        - ii) int
        - iii) long int

The size of the above three variants of int data type are as:

Size

Variants of int	16 bit m/c	32 bit m/c
Unsigned int	2 bytes	4 bytes
signed int	2 bytes	4 bytes

Range of int is given by

Variants of int	16 bit m/c	32 bit m/c
Unsigned int	0 to 2^{16}-1 0 to 65535	0 to 2^{32}-1 0 to 4294967296
signed int	-2^{15} to 2^{15}-1 -32768 to 32767	-2^{31} to 2^{31}-1

bool:

- ➢ A bool is a keyword which is used to define Boolean values in C++ language.
- ➢ Objects of type bool can store only the values true or false.
- ➢ True or false are keywords defined by C++.
- ➢ A non zero value is considered to be true and a zero value is considered to be false.
- ➢ True is converted to 1 and false is converted to 0.

char:

- ➢ A char is a keyword which is used to define character in C++ language.
- ➢ The characters are stored in ASCII format in C++.
- ➢ Each character is associated with unique code called ASCII code.
- ➢ The char datatype occupies 1 byte in both 16 bit and 32 bit machine.
- ➢ Range of signed char is -125 to 125.

➢ Range of unsigned char is 0 to 255.

float:

➢ Float is a keyword which is used to define decimal values in C++.
➢ They are used to represent floating point numbers.
➢ C++ specifies the range of floating point value is 1.2E-38 to 3.4E+38.
➢ The float occupies 4 bytes in 16 bit machine and 8 bytes in 32 bit machine.
➢ The float can hold upto maximum 6 decimal places.

double:

➢ Double is a keyword which is used to define long floating values in C++.
➢ The double can hold upto 15 decimal places.
➢ The double occupies 8 bytes in memory.
➢ C++ specifies the range of double to be 2.3e-308 to 1.7e+308

void:

➢ Void is a keyword which denotes null.
➢ The datatype void is used in declaring the function as returning no value or used to create generic pointers.

string:

➢ Is used to store a sequence of characters.
➢ Is not a built-in type.
➢ Values must be surrounded by double quotes.
➢ To use strings, an additional header file called <string.h> should be included.
➢ It is a pointer which points to character array.
➢ The size of string datatype is 4 bytes.
> **Eg:** string str = "hello"
> Size(str)= 6 bytes
> Length(str)=5

1.2.1 Size and range of different datatypes:

Datatype	Size	Range
int	machine dependent	
Unsigned int		
16 bit	2 bytes	0 to $2^{16}-1$ = 0 to 65535
32 bit	4 bytes	0 to $2^{32}-1$ = 0 to 4294967296

Datatype	Size	Range
Signed int		
16 bit	2 bytes	-2^{15} to 2^{15}-1 = -32768 to 32767
32 bit	4 bytes	2^{31} to 2^{31}-1
Bool	1 byte	True, false True-1 False – 0
Void	Null/ 0 bytes	Null
Char	1 byte	
Unsigned char		0 to 255
Signed char	1 byte	-128 to 127
String	4 bytes Because it is a pointer which points to character array	Length = size(string)-1 Size= size(str)
Float		
16 bit	4 bytes	1.2 E -38 to 3.4E+38
32 bit	8 bytes	Correct to 6 decimal places
Double		
16 bit	8 bytes	2.3 E -308 to 1.7E+308
32bit	8 bytes	Correct to 15 decimal places
Wchar_t	2 bytes	

Table 1.1: Size and Range of datatypes

1.2.2   C++ variables:

- ➢ Variables are containers for storing data values
- ➢ It is the name given to memory locations.
- ➢ How to declare variables?
  - ○ Datatype vname1, vname2,…;
  - ○ Where datatype is one of the basic , derived or user defined datatype.
  - ○ Vname1, vname2 are the names of variables.
    - Eg: int mynum=5;
      - cout<< mynum;
- ➢ Rules for framing variable name:
  - ○ A variable name should start with a letter or underscore and can be followed by any letter or or digit or underscore.
  - ○ Should not include any special character other than underscore.

- o   Should be maximum of 31 character.
- o   A keyword should not be used as variable name.
- ➢   The above rules are applicable in creating array or pointer or function names(identifiers).

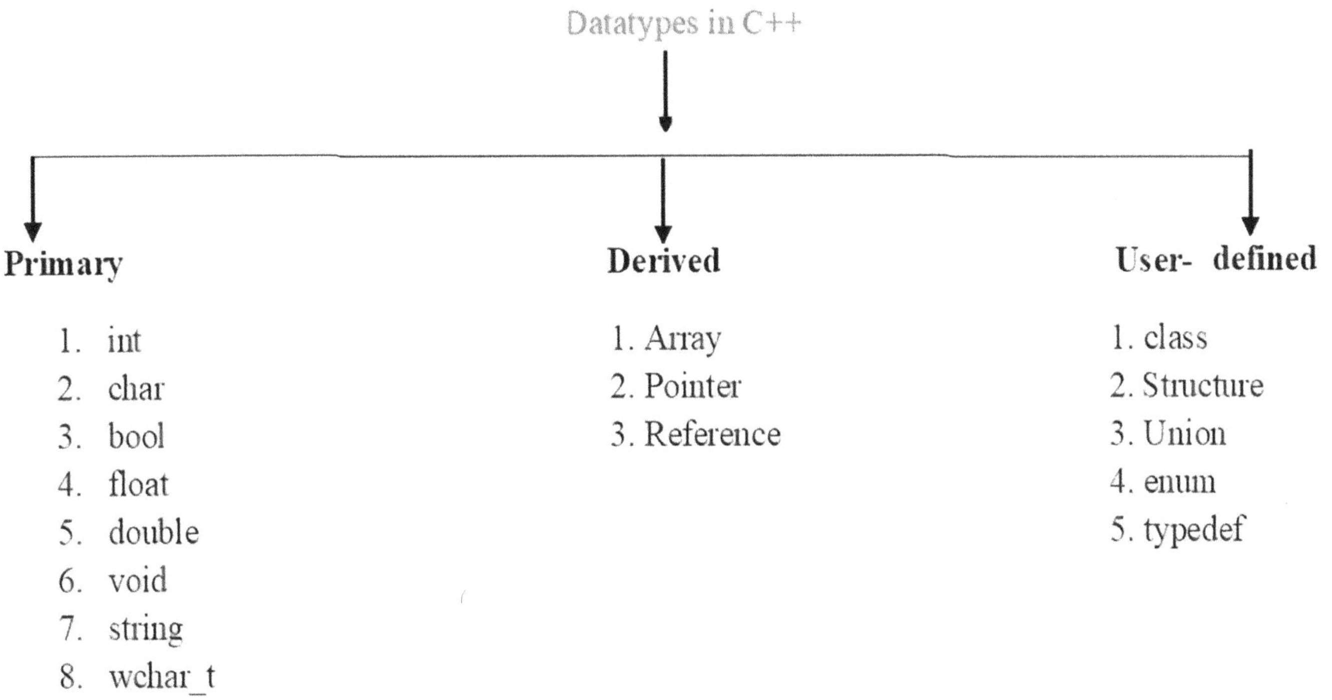

Fig 1.1: *Types of datatypes*

Derived Datatypes:

The datatype that are derived from the primitive or built in datatypes are defined as derived data type.

1.   Array
2.   Pointer
3.   Reference
     are the derived datatype.

User defined datatype:

The datatype defined by user itself are user defined datatype.

1.   Class
2.   Structure
3.   Union
4.   Enum
5.   Typedef
     are the user defined datatype.

1.3 Operators in C++

1. Operator is a symbol which performs | defines the type of operation.
2. An operand is a constant | function | variable.
3. An expression is a combination of operator and operator which returns a value

1.4 Types of operators

Operators are classified into two types based on

1. Number of operands.
2. Type of operation.

1.4.1 Type of operators based on the number of operands:

Based on the number of operands , operators are classified into:

1. Unary operators
2. Binary operators
3. Ternary operators
4. Special operators

1. **Unary operators:**
   An operand which acts on single operand is called unary operator.
   Eg: Unary + , Unary - , Increment (++) or decrement operator(--)

2. **Binary operators:**
   An operand which acts on two operands is called binary operator.
   Eg: Arithmetic, bitwise, logical, relational operators.

3. **Ternary operators:**
   An operand which acts on three operands is called ternary operator.
   Eg: ? and : operator
   Ternary operator is called as conditional operator.

4. **Special operators:**
   :: scope resolution operator
   , comma operator
   Sizeof operator
   ; semicolon operator

1.4.2   Type of operators based on the type of operation being performed:

Based on the type of operation , operators are divided into following types:

1. Arithmetic operators
2. Relational operators
3. Logical operators
4. Bitwise operators
5. Conditional / Ternary operator
6. Increment / Decrement operator
7. Assignment operator
8. Special operator

1.4.3   Arithmetic operators:

- ➢ These operators are used to perform arithmetic or mathematical operations on operands.
- ➢ The different arithmetic operators available in C++ are:
    - a) Addition (+)
    - b) Subtraction (-)
    - c) Division (/)
    - d) Multiplication (*)
    - e) Modulus(%)
    - f)

C++ program to perform simple arithmetic operators:

```cpp
#include<stdio.h>
using namespace std;
int main()
{
    int a, b, res;
    cout<< "enter the values of a and b\n";
    cin>>a>>b;
    cout<<" the sum of a and b is" <<a+b<<endl;
    cout<<" the difference of a and b is" <<a-b<<endl;
    cout<<" the product of a and b is" <<a*b<<endl;
    cout<<" the quotient of a and b is" <<a/b<<endl;
    cout<<" the modulus of a and b is" <<a%b<<endl;
    return 0;
}
```

Output:

```
enter the values of a and b
10
5
the sum of a and b is 15
the difference of a and b is  5
the product of a and b is 150
the quotient of a and b is 2
the modulus of a and b is 0
```

1.4.4   Relational operators:

> The operators that are used for the comparison of the values of two operands and results in either true or false.
> The different relational operators available in C++ are:
>   1. Greater than (>)
>   2. Greater than or equal to (>=)
>   3. Lesser than (<)
>   4. Lesser than or equal to (<=)
>   5. Equal to or comparison operator (==)
>   6. Not equal to (! =)

```
//C++ program to demonstrate the relational operators
#include<iostream>
using namespace std;
int main ()                             output
{
    Int a=10, b=5;
    cout<<a>b<<endl;                    true
    cout<<a<b<<endl;                    false
    cout<<a≥b<<endl;                    true
    cout<<a≤b<<endl;                    false
    cout<<a==b<<endl;                   false
    cout<<a! =b<<endl;                  true
return 0;
}
```

NOTE: The output of relational operator is always true or false.

1.4.5   Logical Operators:

- ➢ Logical operators are used to combine two or more conditions/constraints or to complement the evaluation of the original condition.
- ➢ These operators are used to combine two or more relational operators.
- ➢ The output of logical operators is either true or false.
- ➢ True is nonzero value and false is a zero value.
- ➢ The different logical operators available in C++ are:
    1. Logical AND (&&)
    2. Logical OR (||)
    3. Logical NOT(!)

1. Logical AND (&&)

- ➢ Denoted by && and outputs either true or false.
- ➢ Returns true if both the operands are true, returns false otherwise.

Operand1	Operand 2	Operand1 && operand 2
True (1)	True (1)	True (1)
True (1)	False (0)	False (0)
False (0)	True (1)	False (0)
False (0)	False (0)	False (0)

2. Logical OR (||)

- ➢ Denoted by || and outputs either true or false.
- ➢ Returns false if both the operands are false, returns true otherwise.

Operand1	Operand 2	Operand1 || operand 2
True (1)	True (1)	True (1)
True (1)	False (0)	True (1)
False (0)	True (1)	True (1)
False (0)	False (0)	False (0)

3. Logical NOT(!)

- ➢ Denoted by ! and outputs or returns true or false.
- ➢ This is a unary operator and acts on single operand.
- ➢ Returns true if the operand is false and vice versa.

Operand	! Operand
True(1)	False (0)
False (0)	True (1)

```cpp
//C++ program to illustrate the usage of logical operators
#include<iostream>
using namespace std;
int main()
{
    int a=4, b=5, c=0;
    cout<< " logical AND is"<<" a&& b" << a&&b <<endl;
    cout<< " logical AND is"<<" a&&c" << a&&c <<endl;
    cout<< " logical OR is"<<" a||b" << a||b <<endl;
    cout<< " logical OR is"<<" a|| c" << a&&c<<endl;
    cout<< " logical NOT is"<<" !a" <<   !a <<endl;
    cout<< " logical NOT is"<<" !c" << !c <<endl;
    return 0;
}
```

Output: Tracing (a= 4, b=5, c=0)

```
Logical AND is a&&b True                4&&5=True
logical AND is a&&c False               4&&0=False
logical OR is a||b True                 4||5=True
logical OR is a|| c True                4||0=True
logical NOT is !a False                 !4=False
logical NOT is !c True                  !0=True
```

1.4.6   Bitwise operator

- ➤ Bitwise operators are used to perform bit level operations on the operands.
- ➤ The operands are first converted to bit level and then the calculation is performed on the operands.
- ➤ The arithmetic or mathematical operations can be performed at the bit level for faster processing.
- ➤ The different bitwise operators available in C++ are:
  1. Bitwise AND (&)
  2. Bitwise OR (|)
  3. Bitwise Negate or NOT (~)
  1. Bitwise AND (&):
     - ➤ Denoted by &.
     - ➤ Is a binary operator
     - ➤ Result of bitwise AND is 1 if both the bits are 1 , 0 otherwise.

2. Bitwise OR (|):
    ➢ Denoted by |.
    ➢ Is a binary operator
    ➢ Result of bitwise OR is 0 if both the bits are 0 , 1 otherwise.
3. Bitwise Negate (~):
    ➢ Denoted by ~.
    ➢ Is a unary operator
    ➢ Result of bitwise Not is 0 if the bit is 1 , 1 otherwise.

```cpp
//C++ program to demonstrate the usage of bitwise operator:
#include<iostream>
using namespace std;
int main()
{
        int a=5, b=4, c;
        c = a&b;



        cout<<" a&b=" <<c<<endl;
        c=a| b;



        cout<<" a|b" <<c<<endl;


        c=~a;

        cout<<" ~a" <<c<<endl;
        return 0;
}
```

```
                        TRACING
                   a=5, b=4
                   a = 00000101
                   b = 00000100
                  a&b=00000100

                    a&b=4
                 a=00000101
                     b=00000100
             a|b=00000101

             a|b=5

                   a=00000101
                   c=11111010
                     c=240
```

Output:

```
a&b=4
a|b=5
~a=240
```

1.4.7   Conditional operator:

- Conditional operator operates on three operands.
- Denoted by ? and : symbol
- Syntax:

        exp1 ? exp2 : exp3

- Working:
- The three operands are denoted by exp1, exp2, exp3
- exp1 is evaluated first
- The result of exp1 is either true or false
- If the result of exp1 is true then exp2 gets evaluated.
- If the result of exp1 is false then exp3 gets evaluated.

```cpp
//C++ Program to demonstrate the ternary operator:
#include<iostream>
using namespace std;
int main ()
{
    int a, b,max;
    cout<<" enter the value of a and b\n" <<endl;
    cin>>a>>b;

    max=(a>b)? a: b;
    cout<<"max(a,b)="<<max<<endl;
    return 0;
}
```

Output:

```
enter the value of a and b
10
5
max(a,b)=10
```

Working:

In the above program, we try to find the largest of 2 numbers a and b using ternary operator:

- First, the op1, (a>b) is evaluated.
- If a>b , then max is initialized or assigned with the value a.
    - i.e., if a>b, max=a //exp2 is evaluated.
- If a<b, then max is assigned to value b
    - i.e., if a<b, max=b //exp3 is evaluated.

1.5 Introduction to Branching and Looping statements in C++

C++ supports various branching and looping statements which are discussed as shown in below sections.

1.5.1 Branching Statements in C++

Following are the **decision-making statements** available in C:

1. if Statement
2. if-else Statement
3. Nested if Statement
4. if-else-if Ladder
5. switch Statement
6. Conditional Operator
7. JumpStatements:
     - break
     - continue
     - goto
     - return

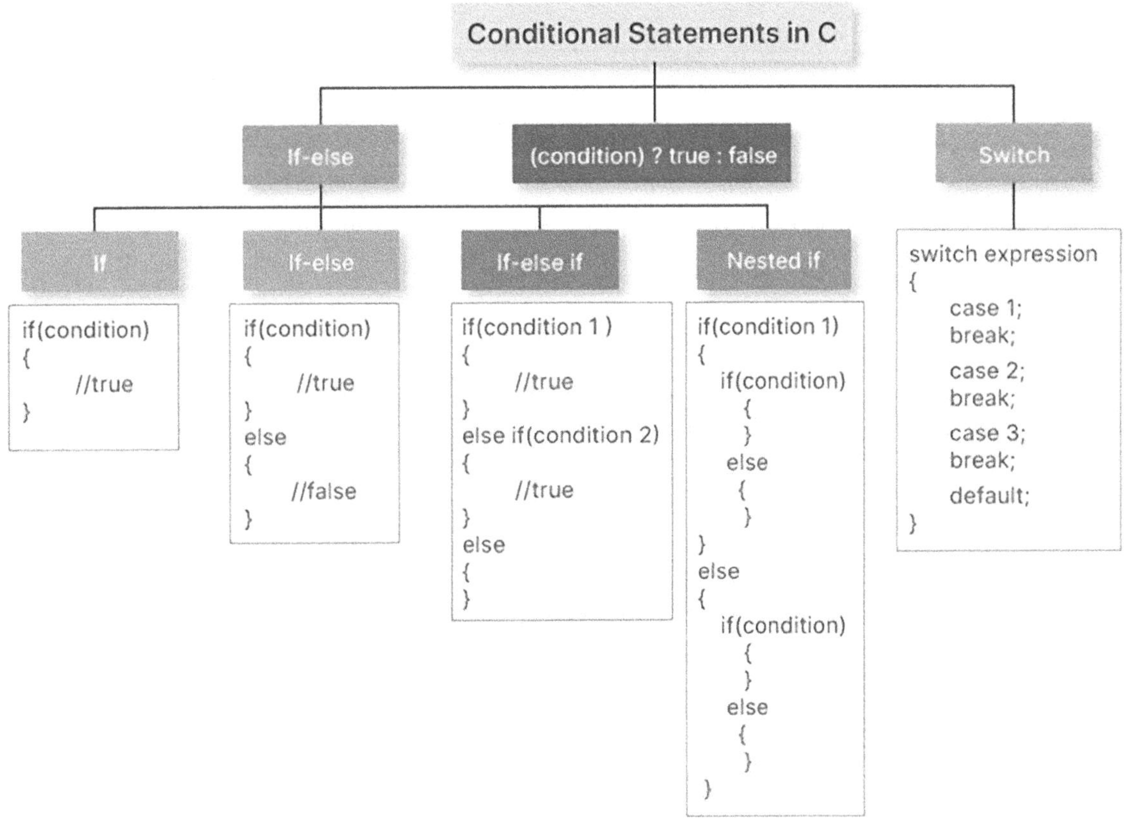

Fig 1.2: Conditional Statements in C and C++

1.5.2 Looping Statements in C++

C++ supports three types of loops

1. for
2. while
3. do while

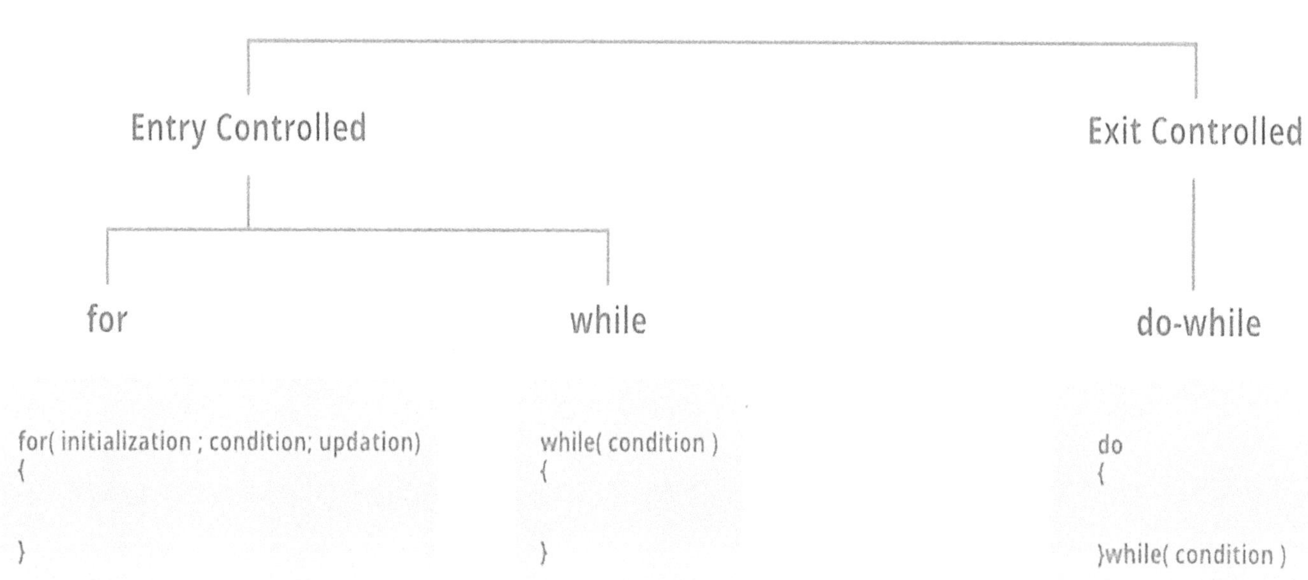

Fig 1.3: Types of Loops in C++

1.5.3 Jump Statements

The jump statements in C++ are discussed in the following sections:

1. Break Statement

- Break statement is used to terminate loop or switch statements.
- It works as shown below:
    - Break statement in switch statement causes the control to terminate the switch statement and the statement following switch statement will be executed.
    - If break statement is executed in a loop, the control comes out of the loop and statement following loop statement will be executed.
- It is used to exit a loop early, breaking out of the enclosing curly braces. Break statement is normally used to terminate a loop when a specific condition is reached.

Syntax:

break;

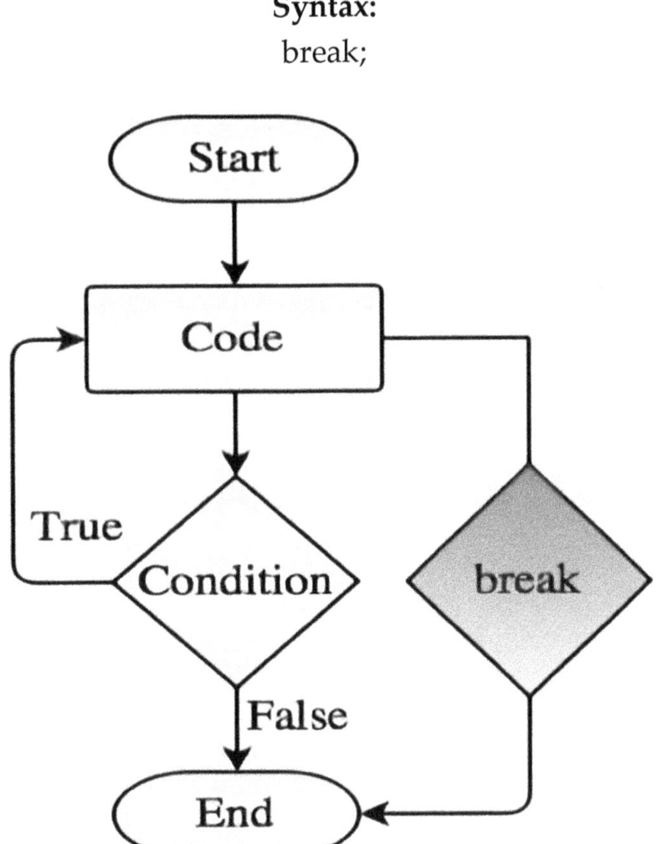

Fig 1.4: *Flow Diagram of Break statement*

Example Program Demonstrating the Break statement's execution

```cpp
#include <iostream>
using namespace std;
int main()
{
    int count = 0;
    do
    {
        cout<<"Value: "<<count<<endl;
        count++;
        if(count>5)
        {
            break;    //terminate the loop
        }
    }
    while(count<10);
    return 0;
}
```

Output:

```
Value: 0
Value: 1
Value: 2
Value: 3
Value: 4
Value: 5
```

2. Continue Statement

- Continue statement skips the remaining code block.
- During execution of a loop, it might be necessary to skip some of the loop statements. In such conditions, continue statement is used.This statement causes the loop to continue with the next iteration.
- It is used to suspend the execution of current loop iteration and transfer control to the loop for the next iteration.

Syntax:

continue;

- **In For Loop,** continue statement causes the conditional test and increment/ decrement statement of the loop gets executed.
- **In While Loop,** continue statement takes control to the condition statement.
- **In Do-While Loop,** continue statement takes control to the condition statement specified in the while loop.

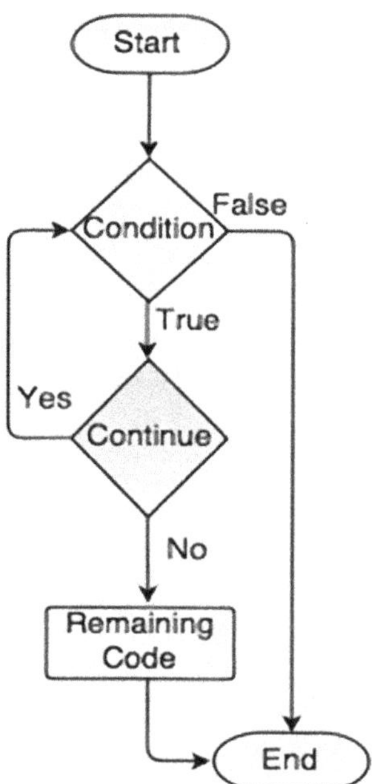

Fig 1.5: Flow Diagram of Continue Statement

Example Program Demonstrating the execution of Continue statement

```cpp
#include <iostream>
using namespace std;
int main()
{
    int count = 0;
    do
    {
        count++;
        if(count>5 && count<10)
            continue;
            cout<<"Value: "<<count<<endl;
    }
    while(count<11);
    return 0;
}
```

Output:

```
Value: 1
Value: 2
Value: 3
Value: 4
Value: 5
Value: 10
Value: 11
```

3. Goto Statement

- Goto statement transfers the current execution of program to some other part. It is used to transfer control to a specified statement in a program.
- It provides an unconditional jump from goto to a labeled statement in the same function.
- It makes difficult to trace the control flow of program and should be avoided in order to make smoother program.

Syntax:

```cpp
goto label;
.
.
.
label: Statement;

goto is a keyword.
```

Label is an identifier that identifies a labeled statement, followed by a colon (:).

- It is used to exit from deeply nested looping statements.
- If we avoid the goto statement, it forces a number of additional tests to be performed.

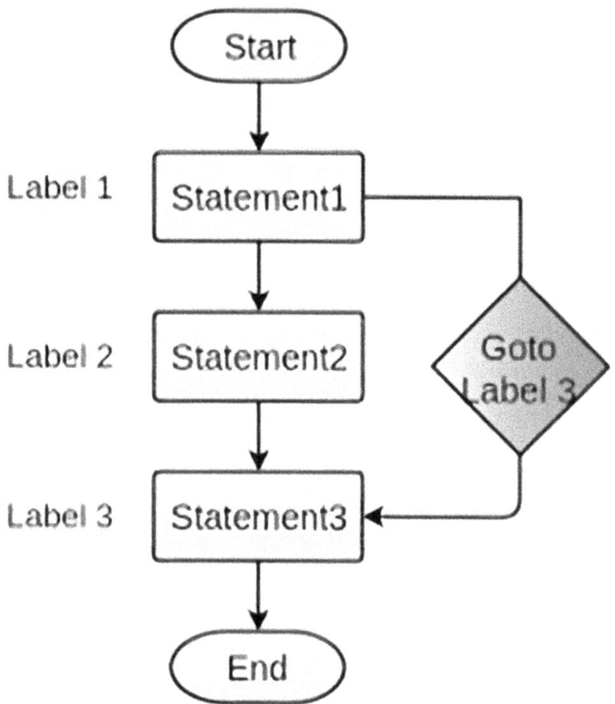

Fig 1.6: *Flow Diagram of Goto Statement*

Example Program Demonstrating the execution of Goto Statement

```cpp
#include <iostream>
using namespace std;
int main ()
{
    int no = 0;
    label1:do
    {
        if( no == 4)
        {
            no = no + 1;     //Skip the iteration
            goto label1;
        }
        cout << "Value : " << no << endl;
        no = no + 1;
    }while( no < 5 );
    return 0;
}
```

Output:

```
Value : 0
Value : 1
Value : 2
Value : 3
Value : 5
```

CHAPTER - 2

Chapter 2

Introduction to OOPS

Introduction

The C++ language provides object-oriented programming approach where the programs are written using the concept of classes and objects. This language also provides static and dynamic memory allocation methods where the memory for variables in the program can be allocated using new and delete operators. These operators can be used to create dynamic arrays. The relation between pointers and arrays and how the arrays can be referred to as pointers is an important topic that helps in understanding the further topics of creating arrays using the dynamically allocation operators. The C++ language provides the special function called constructors and destructors.

Structure

The chapter covers the following topics:

- **OOP Concepts:**
    - Features of object-oriented programming
    - Classes and objects
    - Introduction to data structures
    - Dynamic memory allocation operators
- **OOP concepts and features:**
    - Constructors and its types
    - Destructors
- **Arrays:**
    - Introduction
    - Types of arrays
    - Dynamic arrays.

Objectives:

After reading this chapter, the reader will come to know about data structures and their types in C++ language. The dynamic memory management in C++, concept of arrays and pointers followed by dynamic data structures and also the concept of special member functions constructors and destructors will be discussed in this chapter. This will help the reader to write efficient programs using dynamic arrays and dynamic data structures.

2.1   Features of Object-Oriented Programming

Following are the features of object-oriented programming:

Encapsulation:

Encapsulation refers to binding the data and code in one single entity. This feature of OOPs helps in preventing data from unauthorized access. In other words, it helps in data security.

Inheritance:

Is a feature of OOPs where the property of one class is inherited to the other class. The class from which the properties are inherited is called base class and the other class which derives or inherits the property of base class is called derived class or sub class.

Polymorphism:

Polymorphism is a feature of OOPs which exhibits the feature of "one interface multiple methods". This feature is implemented in C++ using function overloading, operator overloading and function overriding.

Data Security:

The data is secure in object-oriented programming language. This is achieved using access specifiers in C++ (public, private and protected).

Data abstraction:

Hiding the implementation details from the user is referred as data abstraction. The implementation details are hidden from the user in C++ language.

2.2   Classes and Objects

The classes and objects in C++ are defined as in the following sections

2.2.1   Class in C++

A class in C++ is a blueprint for creating objects. A class defines data (variables) and functions (methods) that operate on that data. Unlike C programming language, classes in C++ is a combination of data and methods or functions.

```
Syntax to create class in C++
class c_name
{
      access_specifiers:
            datatype1 v1;
            datatype2 v2;
            ....;
            ....;
            datatypen vn;
      access_specifiers:
            func1()
            {
                  .....
            }
            func2()
            {
                  .....
            }
};
```

class c_name → Defines a class named c_name.

Access Specifiers (private, public, protected)

- Control access to data and functions.
- Example:
    - private: → Members are accessible only within the class.
    - public: → Members are accessible from outside the class.
    - protected: → Used in inheritance (accessible in derived classes).
- Data Members (v1, v2, ..., vn)
    - These are variables inside the class that store data related to objects.
- Member Functions (func1(), func2())
    - These define the behavior of the class.
    - Functions operate on the data members.

2.2.2   Access Specifiers in C++:

The data members and member functions of a class can be accessed using access specifiers. C++ supports three types of access specifiers. They are:

1. public
2. private
3. protected

public access specifier in C++

- public is a keyword in C++.
- If the data members and member functions of a class are declared as public, they can be accessed by non-member functions defined outside the class.
- The data members of a class can be accessed by the member functions of a class irrespective of whether they are declared as private or protected.

private access specifier in C++

- private is a keyword in C++.
- If the data members and member functions of a class are declared as private, they cannot be accessed by non-member functions defined outside the class.
- The data members and member functions of a class are private by default.

protected access specifier in C++:

- protected is a keyword in C++.
- If the data members and member functions of a class are declared as protected, they cannot be accessed by non-member functions defined outside the class. But can be accessed by the inherited members of a class.
- The data members and member functions of a class are private by default.

```
C++ Program to demonstrate the usage of access specifiers in C++
class example
{
    public:
        int a;
    private:
        int b;
    protected:
        int c;
    public:
        void result ()
        {
            a=10;
            b=20;
            c=30;
            cout<<a<<b<<c;
        }
};
void nmresult()
```

```
{
    a=10;
    b=20;
    c=30;
    cout<<a<<b<<c;
}
int main()
{
    1. example obj1;
    2. obj1.result();
    3. nmresult();
    4. return 0;
}
```

Results:

Observe the following points from the above program:

- Execution starts from function main
- When the statement 1 is executed, an object named obj1 of class example is created.
- When the statement 2 is executed, the member function result() is invoked. Since result is a member function of a class, the corresponding values of a, b and c are displayed.
- When the statement 3 is executed, the control is transferred to the non-member function nmresult(). Since the variable a is declared under public, a=10 is executed and is not illegal. The variable b is declared under private and cannot be accessed from the non-member function and is considered to be illegal. Similarly protected also cannot be accessed from this non-member function. Hence error messages will be displayed and program will not get executed.

2.3   Introduction to data structures

A data structure is a particular way of organizing data in a computer effectively. The idea here is to reduce the space and time complexities of different tasks.

Data structure affects the design of both the structural and functional aspects of a program.

Algorithm + Data Structure = Program

Data structures are the building blocks of a program. The selection of a particular data structure will help the programmer to design more efficient programs as the complexity of the program increases.

The representation of a particular data structure in the memory of a computer is called a storage structure. The data structure should be represented so that it utilizes maximum efficiency. It can be represented in both the main and auxiliary memory of the computer. A storage structure representation in auxiliary memory is often called a file structure.

Data Structure = Organized data + Operations

2.4 Classification of data structure

Fig 1.1 shows how data structures in C can be classified. In C language, we have two types of data structures. The first one is *primitive data structures* which are further divided into int, float, char, double and void based on the type of data they hold. The other type of data structure is *non primitive data structure* which are further divided into linear and non-linear data structure which are explained in brief in the upcoming sections.

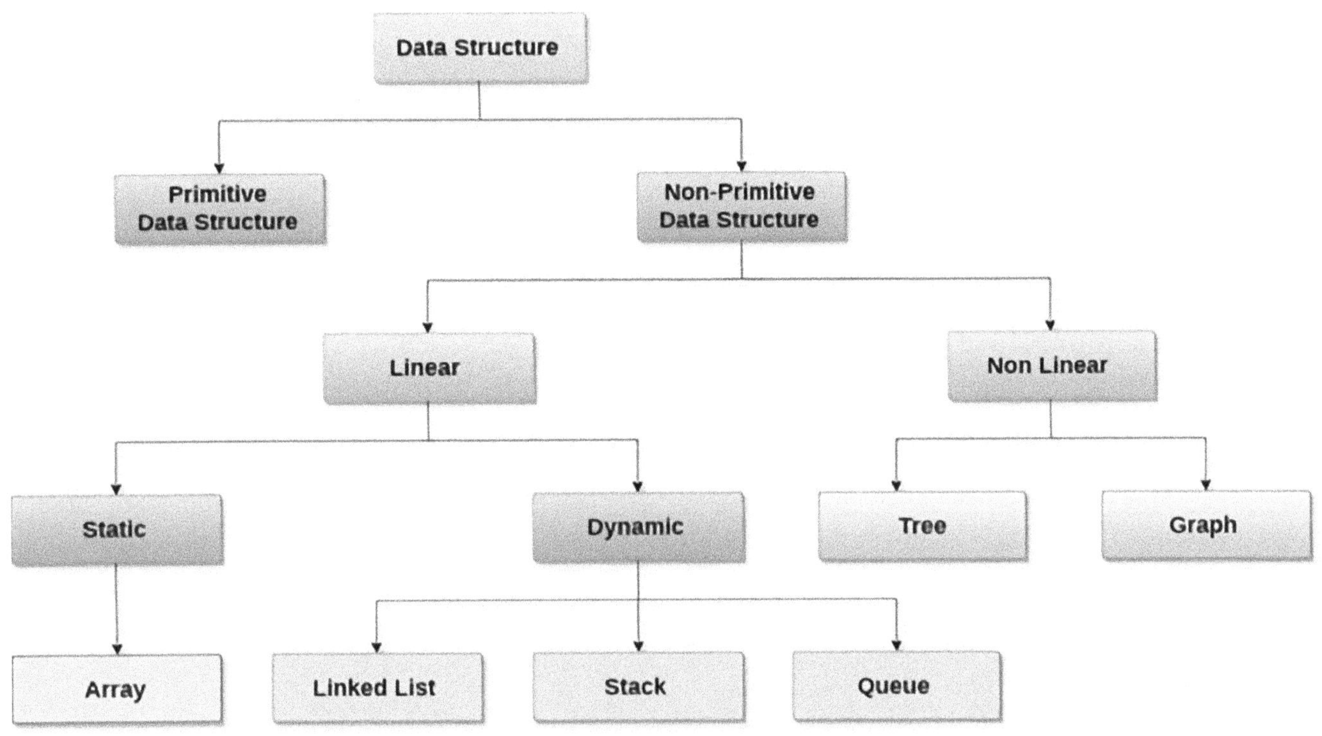

Fig 2.1: Classification of data structure

The data structures are broadly divided into two categories, which are discussed as follows:

2.4.1 Primitive data structures

The data structures which can be directly manipulated by machine instructions are called primitive data structures. These are basic data structures and are directly operated at a primitive level and are divided based on the type of data they hold.

For example: integers (int), floating point numbers (float), characters (char), double or long floating point number, pointers to store addresses and more.

2.4.2   Non primitive data structures

The data structures that are derived from the primitive data structures or the data structures that cannot be manipulated or operated by machine-level instructions are called non primitive data structures. The focus of these data structures is on forming a set of elements that is either homogenous or heterogeneous. Based on the arrangement and structure of data, we can divide the data structures into two categories:

- o   Linear data structures
- o   Non linear data structures

2.4.3   Linear data structures

The data structure where the arrangement of the data is done linearly or sequentially and also preserves a linear connection among its data elements is known as linear data structure. Based on memory allocation, the linear data structures are classified into two types:

Static data structure:

Data structures having a fixed size are known as static data structures. The amount of memory to be allocated for these data structures is fixed during compilation time and cannot be altered during execution time. However, the data stored in them can be altered for these data structures.

For example: Array is an example of static data structure as it has a fixed size.

Dynamic data structures:

In these data structures, the amount of memory to be allocated is fixed and allocated during execution time or run time. The size or amount of memory varies during the run time of the code. That is, the size and data elements stored in these data structures can be changed by the user at the run time of the code.

For example, stacks, queues, and linked lists are examples of dynamic data structures.The linear data structures(static or dynamic) can be further classified into:

- o   Arrays
- o   Files
- o   String
- o   Stack
- o   List
- o   Queues

Arrays: An array is a data structure which is a collection of homogenous data elements described by a single name. Each element of an array is referenced by a subscripted variable, called subscript or index, enclosed within [ ].The different types of arrays are:

Single dimensional array or 1D array: If an element in an array is referenced by single subscript, then the array is known as 1 D array. It has only one row of data elements.

- Two-dimensional array or 2D array:

If two subscripts are required to reference an element in an array, then the array is known as 2D array. Here the array consists of many rows and columns of data elements also known as matrix.

Multi-dimensional arrays: The arrays whose elements are referenced by two or more subscripts are called multidimensional arrays. It is array of arrays.

The applications of arrays are as follows:

- List of data elements of the same data type can be stored.
- The other data structures like stacks, queues, and more can be implemented using arrays.

Linked lists: Linked lists are an example of linear data structure where data elements in this data structure are represented by the collection of nodes where each node has some information or data connected using links or pointers.

Each node in the linked list contains two fields: the information field or the info field or data field, which consists of the actual data, and the pointer field which consists of the address of the subsequent nodes in the list. The pointer field is also called the link field and is pictorially represented as shown in the Fig below:

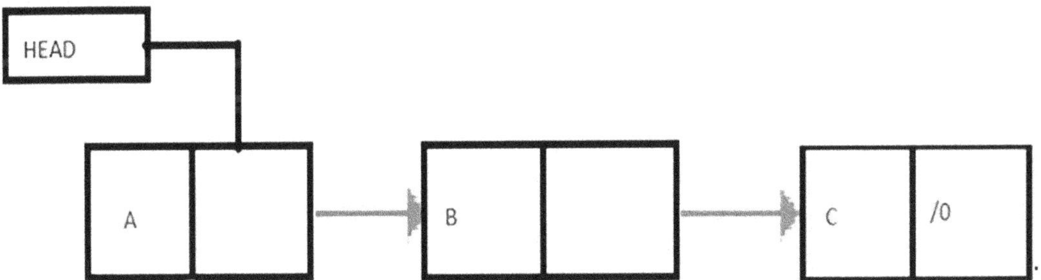

Fig 2.2: Pictorial representation of linked list

Linked lists are classified into:

- Singly linked list
- Doubly linked list
- Circular linked list

The application of linked lists are as follows:

- Helps to implement data structures like stacks, queues, or trees of predefined tasks.
- Circular linked list is used to implement operating system algorithms like round robin.
- Doubly linked list is used to implement forward and backward buttons in a browser, which helps to move forward and backward in the opened pages of a website.

Stacks: A stack is a linear data structure that follows either the Last In First Out (LIFO) principle or the First In Last Out (FILO) principle that allows operations like insertion (push), deletion (pop), and display. The insertion and deletion happen at the same end, called the top of the stack.

The applications of stack are as follows:

- Stack acts as a temporary storage for recursive functions.
- Stacks are used in managing function calls.
- Stacks are used in converting expressions and evaluation of expressions.
- Stacks can be used to reverse a string.

These will be discussed in detail later in the chapter.**Queues:** A queue is a linear data structure that follows the FIFO principle to manipulate the data elements. The operations like insertion (Enqueue), deletion (dequeue), and display can be implemented using queues.

The applications of queue are as follows:

- Queues are used in BFS operations in graphs.
- Queues are used in implementing the job scheduler operations of OS.
- CPU, job and disk scheduling are possible through queues.

2.4.4 Non-linear data structures

The data structure where the arrangement of data elements is not in sequential order are referred as non linear data structures.

Trees

A tree is a non-linear data structure containing a collection of nodes such that each node of the tree stores a data and the address of the subsequent nodes.

Trees can be classified into Binary Tree, BST, AVL Tree, B–Tree

The applications of trees are as follows:

- Used to generate Huffman's code.
- Expression trees are used in solving expressions

Graphs

A graph is a set consisting of set of vertices V and set of edges E, as shown below:

$$G = (V,E)$$

The applications of graphs are as follows:

- Used to represent routes and networks in communication networks.
- Used to display routes in GPS.

2.5 Dynamic memory management in C++

The memory in C++ language is allocated only during execution time. But the amount of memory to be allocated may or may not be known during compilation time. Based on whether the memory to be allocated is known or not known, the memory allocation in C++ is divided into two types which are discussed in the upcoming sections.

2.5.1 Static memory allocation

In this type of memory allocation, the required memory is allocated to the variables at the beginning of the program. Here, the memory to be allocated is fixed and is determined by the compiler at the compile time itself.

For example:

1. int a, b;
2. float arr[5],fl;

When the above statements are compiled:

- 2 bytes for both the variables a and b will be allocated.

The second statement will allocate 20 bytes to the array arr (5 elements of floating point type that is 5*4) and 4 bytes for the variable f.The properties of static memory allocation are as follows:

- Stack memory is used here.
- Memory cannot be changed while executing a program.
- Static memory allocation is fast and saves running time.
- It is less efficient as compared to dynamic memory allocation.
- The allocation process is simple.
- The memory to be allocated during execution time is fixed during compilation time only.

Advantages of static memory allocation are as follows:

- The memory is allocated during compile time.
- It is easy to use.
- It uses a stack data structure
- The execution time is efficiently controlled.

Drawbacks of static memory allocation are as follows:

- This allocation method leads to memory wastage.
- Memory cannot be changed while executing a program.
- Memory requirements must be known in prior.
- If memory is not required, it cannot be freed.

The drawbacks of static memory allocation can be overcome using dynamic memory allocation.

2.5.2   Dynamic memory allocation

In dynamic memory allocation, the memory to be allocated is fixed and allocated during execution time. It makes efficient use of memory by allocating the required amount whenever needed. It helps in allocating memory when we cannot predict the memory requirements.

Properties of dynamic memory allocation:

- Memory is allocated during run time.
- Memory can be allocated and released at any time.
- Heap memory is used here.
- Dynamic memory allocation is slow.
- It is more efficient as compared to static memory allocation.
- The allocation process is simple.

2.6   Dynamic memory allocation operators in C++

The dynamic memory management in C++ can be implemented using the following operators in C++.

    new
    delete

The first three functions are used for memory allocation and the last function free() is used for memory deallocation

2.6.1   Allocating block of memory

Memory can be allocated using new operator. Using delete operator, memory can be deallocated.

Let us talk about these operators in detail now:

2.6.2   new operator

new operator is used to allocate a block of memory dynamically

Syntax:

```
datatype *ptr;
ptr = new datatype;
```

where,

- datatype: can be any of the basic or user-defined datatype.
- ptr: name of the pointer variable

new operator returns

- address of the block of memory allocated.

The following steps are performed when the new opeator is executed:

1. Memory is allocated from the heap.
2. Memory is not modified or otherwise cleared.
3. If the memory is available, it initializes memory to the pointer variable. The first byte's address is returned.

For example:

```
int *ptr;
ptr = new int;
```

Here:

- ptr is a pointer of type int.
- On execution of this statement, memory space equivalent to the size of an 'int' byte is allocated, and address of the first byte is assigned to the pointer variable 'ptr' of type 'int'.
- It is always better to check whether the memory allocation is successful or not before we use the newly allocated memory pointer.

For example:

```
int *ptr;
ptr= new int;
*ptr = 50;
cout<<*ptr
```

When the above sequence is executed, 50 is displayed.

Program showing the usage of new operator

The program below shows how new operator can be implemented :

```
#include<iostream>
using namespace std;
#include<stdlib.h>
int main()
{
        int *ptrint;
        float *ptrfloat;

        ptr=new int;
        ptrfloat= new float;
```

```
        *ptrint=10;
        *ptrfloat=10.5;

        cout<<"ptrint="<<*ptrint<<endl;
        cout<<"ptrfloat="<<*ptrfloat<<endl;

        delete ptrint;
        delete ptrfloat;

}
```

Output:

```
ptrint=10
ptrfloat=10.5
```

Observe the below points when the above program is executed,

- The compiler reserves the space for the variable ptr in the memory.
- Using the new operator, we can request memory to be reserved.
- The specified blocks of memory may be allocated or may not be allocated.
- If allocated successfully, the address of first byte is returned.

2.6.3 Syntax to allocate and initialize a variable using new operator

The syntax to allocate a memory and initialize the memory allocated using new operator is

Syntax:

```
        datatype *ptr;
        ptr=new datatype(value);
```

This syntax is used to allocate a memory and the memory allocated will be initialized to "value".

```
The program below shows how new operator can be implemented to initialize the
memory allocated:
#include<iostream>
using namespace std;
#include<stdlib.h>
int main()
{
        int *ptrint;
        float *ptrfloat;
```

```
        ptr=new int(10);
        ptrfloat= new float(10.5);

        cout<<"ptrint="<<*ptrint<<endl;
        cout<<"ptrfloat="<<*ptrfloat<<endl;

        delete ptrint;
        delete ptrfloat;
}
```

Output:

```
ptrint=10
ptrfloat=10.5
```

2.6.4   new operator to allocate multiple blocks of memory

Multiple blocks of memory can be allocated using new operator. The syntax to allocate multiple blocks of memory using new operator is shown below:

Syntax:

```
        datatype *ptr;
        ptr=new datatype[size];
```

where,

- datatype: can be any of the basic or user-defined datatype.
- ptr: name of the pointer variable
- size: number of blocks of memory to be allocated

Program showing the usage of new operator to allocate multiple blocks of memory:

```
#include<iostream>
using namespace std;
#include<stdlib.h>
int main()
{
        int i,n;
        int *ptr;

        cout<<"enter the number elements"<<endl;
        cin>>n;
```

```cpp
    ptr=new int[n];

    cout<<"enter n elements"<<endl;
    for(i=0;i<n;i++)
    {
        cin>>ptr[i];
    }

    cout<<"the given elements are"<<endl;
    for(i=0;i<n;i++)
    {
        cout<<*(ptr+i);
    }

    delete[] ptr;

    return 0;
}
```

Output:

```
Enter the number of elements
5

Enter n elements
10 20 30 40 50

The given elements are
10
20
30
40
50
```

2.6.5 delete operator

The delete operator is used to deallocate or free the allocated block of memory which is allocated by using the new operator.

It is the responsibility of the programmer to deallocate the memory whenever it is not required by the program.

Syntax:

```
delete ptr;
ptr=NULL;
```

After deallocating the memory using new operator delete the memory allocated using delete operator.

Syntax to delete multiple blocks of memory allocated dynamically using new operator

```
delete[ ] ptr;
```

Sample program to illustrate the usage of delete operator:
```
#include<iostream>
using namespace std;
#include<stdlib.h>
int main()
{
    int *ptr;
    ptr=new int;
    *ptr=10;
    delete ptr;
    return 0;
}
```

Sample program to illustrate the usage of delete operator to delete multiple blocks of memory:
```
#include<iostream>
using namespace std;
#include<stdlib.h>
int main()
{
    int *ptr;
    ptr=new int[5];
    for(i=0;i<n;i++)
    {
        *(ptr+i)=i*i;
        cout<<*(ptr+i)<<endl;
    }
    delete[] ptr;
    return 0;
}
```

Sample program to illustrate the usage of delete function:

```cpp
#include<iostream>
using namespace std;
#include<stdlib.h>
int main()
{
    int *a;
    a=new int;
    *a=100;

    a=new int;
    *a=200;

    delete a;

    return 0;
}
```

2.7   Constructors

Constructors are the special member functions whose name is that of the class name. They may or may not take parameters. Constructors are automatically called when the object is created. It is not necessary to call the constructors explicitly. It appears as a member function of each class whether defined explicitly by the programmer or not.

Syntax of constructor is

```
<class_name> <parameter_list>
```

Constructors are used to initialize data members of a class. It guarantees the initialization of data members of a class.

Types of Constructors:

C++ supports three types of constructors and they are

1. Default Constructor
2. Parameterized Constructor
3. Copy Constructor

2.7.1   Default Constructor:

Constructor with zero or no arguments are referred as default constructors. They are also called as zero argument constructors

Example program to demonstrate the default constructor:

```cpp
#include<iostream>
Using namespace std;
class Example
{
    public:
            int a;
            int b;
    Example()
    {
            a=10;
            b=20;
    }
    void result()
    {
            cout<<"a="<<a<<endl;
            cout<<"b="<<b<<endl;
    }
};
int main()
{
    Example obj1;
    obj1.result()
    return 0;
}
```

Observe the following points from the above program:

1. Variables a and b are the data members of class Example.
2. Example() is the default constructor defined. The name of the function is same as that of the class name. The function does not take any parameters. The variables or the data members a and b are initialized to 10 and 20 respectively.
3. The function result() is also a member function of a class which will display the values of a and b
4. In the function main(), an object obj1 is created which is of type Example.
5. As soon as the object obj1 is created, the default constructor of the class is called automatically and the values of a and b are initialized to 10 and 20 respectively. We did not call or invoke the constructor explicitly. The constructors are called implicitly by the compiler and we need not write any statements to invoke the constructor

2.7.2 Parameterized Constructors

A constructor that takes one or more arguments is called parameterized constructor. Unlike default constructors, these constructors are used to initialize different objects with different initial values. These constructors are automatically invoked when an object with parameters is created.

These constructors can be overloaded. When an object is created with one parameter, the parameterized constructor with one parameter is invoked. When an object is created with two parameters is created, parameterized constructor with two parameters is invoked.

C++ Program to demonstrate the usage of parameterized constructor:

```cpp
#include<iostream>
Using namespace std;
class Example
{
    public:
        int a;
        int b;
        int c;
    Example()
    {
        a=10;
        b=20;
        c=30;
        cout<<"a="<<a<<endl;
        cout<<"b="<<b<<endl;
        cout<<"c="<<c<<endl;
    }
    Example(int m,int n)
    {
        a=m;
        b=n;
        cout<<"a="<<a<<endl;
        cout<<"b="<<b<<endl;

    }
    Example(int g)
    {
        c=g;
        cout<<"c="<<c<<endl;
    }
};
```

```cpp
int main()
{
    cout<<"default constructor is invoked"<<endl;
    Example obj1;
    cout<<"parameterized constructor with one parameter is invoked"<<endl;
    Example obj2(10);
    cout<<"parameterized constructor with two parameter is invoked"<<endl;
    Example obj3(22,29);
    return 0;
}
```

Output:

```
default constructor is invoked
a=10
b=20
c=30
parameterized constructor with one parameter is invoked
c=10
parameterized constructor with two parameter is invoked
a=22
b=29
```

2.7.3 Copy Constructor

Copy Constructor is a special type of parameterized constructor using which one object can be copied into another object. This is normally used to initialize object with the values of already existing object.

2.7.4 Destructors

Just as constructors are used to initialize the data members of a class, destructors are the special member functions which are used to de-initialize the data members of the class. These functions are special because the name of these functions is same as that of the class name but precede with a ~ symbol. The destructors are automatically invoked when an object is about to go out of scope.

2.8 Arrays

An array in C++ is a collection of multiple values of the same data type stored in contiguous memory locations. Arrays allow you to store multiple values under a single variable name and access them using an index.

Why Use Arrays?

- Stores multiple values using a single variable.
- Faster access because data is stored in contiguous memory locations.
- Easier iteration using loops (e.g., for and while).
- More efficient than creating multiple variables separately.

1. Declaring an Array in C++

The basic syntax for declaring an array is:

```
datatype array_name[size];
```

2. Initializing an Array

You can initialize an array at the time of declaration.

```
int numbers[5] = {10, 20, 30, 40, 50};   // Array with predefined values
```

3. Accessing Array Elements

Array elements are accessed using **index numbers**, starting from 0.

```
Example: Accessing Elements
#include <iostream>
using namespace std;
int main()
{
    int numbers[3] = {10, 20, 30};
    cout << "First element: " << numbers[0] << endl;   // 10
    cout << "Second element: " << numbers[1] << endl;  // 20
    cout << "Third element: " << numbers[2] << endl;   // 30
    return 0;
}
```

Types of Arrays in C++

C++ supports different types of arrays:

(a) One-Dimensional Array

A simple list of elements.

```
Example:
int arr[3] = {1, 2, 3};
```

(b) Multi-Dimensional Array (2D Array)

A **2D array** is like a table (rows and columns).

```
Example: 2D Array
#include <iostream>
using namespace std;
int main()
{
    int matrix[2][3] = { {1, 2, 3}, {4, 5, 6} };
    cout << "Element at row 1, col 2: " << matrix[1][2] << endl; // Output: 6
    return 0;
}
```

2.9 Dynamic Arrays

The arrays which are created using the dynamically allocated operator new are referred as dynamic arrays.

The concept of dynamic arrays are explained in the previous subsections.

2.10 Pointers

A pointer is a variable that holds the address of another variable.

Let us now discuss how to declare a pointer variable and access variables through pointers:

- Declare a data variable: int a;
- Declare a pointer variable: int *ptr;
- Initialize a pointer variable: ptr = &a;
- Access data using pointer variable: printf("%d",*ptr);

2.11 Pointers and arrays

Consider the following array declaration:

```
int a[5]={1,2,3,4,5};
```

The above declaration informs the compiler to allocate 5 memory locations and initialize memory locations with initial values as shown below:

<table>
<tr><td>0200</td></tr>
</table>

a

&a[ ]	&a[0]	&a[1]	&a[2]	&a[3]	&a[4]
Address	0200	0202	0204	0206	0208
Value	1	2	3	4	5
a[ ] **Accessed**	a[0]	a[1]	a[2]	a[3]	a[4]

Fig 2.3: Representation of Array

The value 0200 stored in array a cannot be changed, because once the memory is allocated, the variable a contains 0200 which is the starting address of 0th item.

It is clear from above that a and &a[0] are same.

$$a===============\&a[0]================(a+0)$$

Fig 1.24:

Consider the code snippet below:

```
int a[5]={1,2,3,4,5};
cout<<a;
cout<<&a[0];
```

Here the output is:

```
0200  The above statements are equivalent and return the address of a
0200  We can use either the array name a by itself or use &a[0].
```

What is the output of the following program?

```
#include<iostream>
using namespace std;
#include<stdlib.h>
int main()
{
        int a[5]={1,2,3,4,5};
        cout<<a<<” “<<&a[0]<<” “ <<a+0<<endl;
        return 0;
}
```

Output

```
0200    0200    0200
```

Tracing

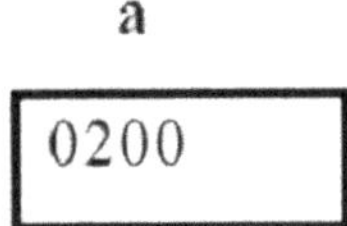

a

a[5]	1	2	3	4	5
Address	0200	0202	0204	0206	0208
&a[ ]	&a[0]	&a[1]	&a[2]	&a[3]	&a[4]

***Fig 2.4:** Representation of Array*

The starting address of the array is called as a base address.

How to access address of each element of an array?

- Address operator with index: &a[i]
- Base address with index: a+i

For example:

&a[0] is same as a+0
&a[1] is same as a+1
&a[2] is same as a+2
&a[3] is same as a+3
&a[4] is same as a+4
&a[0] is same as a+0

In general,

a+i	i+a	&a[i]	&i[a]	are same

***Fig 2.5:** Address of array a*

*(a+i)	*(i+a)	a[i]	i[a]	*&a[i]	*&i[a]	are same

***Fig 2.6:** Values of array a.*

Program to illustrate the above concept:

```c
#include<stdio.h>
int main()
{
int a[5]={1,2,3,4,5};
int i=3;
cout<<*(&a[i])<<" "<<a[i]<<" " <<*(a+i)<<" " <<*(i+a)<<" "i[a]<<" "<<
*&i[a]<<endl;

return 0;
}
```

Output

4 4 4 4 4 4

TRACING:

The tracing of the above program along with memory representation is as shown below:

a

0200

&a[i]	Address	Value	a[i]
&a[0]	0200	1	a[0]
&a[1]	0202	2	a[1]
&a[2]	0204	3	a[2]
&a[3]	0206	4	a[3]
&a[4]	0208	5	a[4]

Fig 2.7: Tracing of the above program

Value	Equal to	Output
*(&a[i])	a[3]	4
a[i]	a[3]	4
a+i	a+3	4
i+a	3+a	4
i[a]	a[3]	4
*&i[a]	a[3]	4

Fig 2.8: *Tracing of the above program*

2.12   Pointers and one-dimensional arrays

Address of each element of an array can be calculated using:

Address of a[i]=Base address + Index of item + sizeof(datatype)

Datatype can be any of the basic datatype such as **int**, float, char, double etc.,

For example:

&a[i] = base address + index of item *sizeof(int)
&a[3]= 0200+3*2 ===== 0206

```
Program to implement pointer arithmetic operation
#include<stdio.h>
int main()
{
int a[5] = {1,2,3,4,5};
int *ptr;
int i,sum;

ptr=a;
sum=0;

for(i=0;i<4;i++)
```

```
{
            sum=sum+(*ptr);           //same as sum=sum + *(ptr++)
            ptr++;
}

printf("sum of all numbers %d\n",sum);

return 0;
}
```

Output

```
sum of all numbers 15
```

Program takes a value and multiplies it against each element of array a:

```
#include<stdio.h>
int main()
{
      int a[]={1,2,3,4,5},i;
      int *ptr, value;

      ptr=a;
      value=2;

      for(i=0;i<5;i++)
      {
            *ptr= *ptr  * value;//same as *ptr++ = *ptr *(value);
            ptr++;
      }

      printf("after multiplying \n");

      for(i=0;i<5;i++)
      {
            printf("%d\n",*ptr);
            ptr++;
      }

      return 0;
}
```

Output

```
2
4
6
8
10
```

2.13 Exercises

1. What is a data structure?
2. How many types of data structures are there?
3. What are the major applications of data structures?
4. Where are data structures used?
5. What is an array?
6. What is a multi-dimensional array?
7. What is a stack?
8. What is a linked-list data structure?
9. Are linked-list data structures linear or non-linear?
10. What is a recursive data structure?
11. Are linked-list data structures more efficient than arrays?
12. How can you find the largest or the smallest integer in an unsorted integer array?
13. What is an array data structure?
14. How does the quicksort algorithm sort an integer array in place?
15. How can you find duplicates in an array?
16. Is it possible to change the array size during the run time?
17. What is the default value of an array?
18. Explain the anonymous array.
19. Explain the steps for declaring multi-dimensional arrays in Java.
20. Do we have 3-dimensional arrays in C?
21. How do you intersect two sorted arrays?
22. How do dynamic arrays work?
23. What is pointer to an array? Explain with example.
24. Explain the dynamic memory allocation functions available in C.
25. What is the purpose of new ? Explain with an example.
26. What is the purpose of free ? Explain with an example.
27. What is dangling pointer? Explain with an example.
28. Discuss the classification of data structures.
29. Define structures. Discuss the method of defining structures.

30. Discuss the concept of structures and pointers.
31. What happens if the following code is executed?
    - int *ptr;
    - ptr=new int(5);
32. Discuss how realloc can be used to extend the memory from 25 to 35 bytes in the above code?

2.14   List of programs

1. Design and develop a C Program to find sum and product of elements in a given array
2. Design and develop a C program to find largest and smallest element in an array
3. Design and develop a C program to multiply two matrices of order m*n.
4. Design and develop a C program to print array in reverse order. Implement the same using dynamic arrays
5. Design and develop a C program for finding the number of even and odd numbers in an arrays.
6. Design a C++ program to implement linear search to search for an element in an array.
7. Design a C++ program to implement binary search.
8. Design a C++ program to merge two arrays of size a and b into a single array.
9. Design a C++ program to find mean and median of two sorted arrays
10. Design and develop a C program to reverse an array
11. Design a C++ program to sort elements using merge sort.
12. Design a C++ program to sort elements using quick sort.
13. Design a C++ program to sort elements using selection sort.
14. Design a C++ program to sort elements using insertion sort.
15. Design a C++ program to sort elements using bubble sort.
16. Design a C++ program to print the smallest and least element in an array.
17. Design a C++ program to find the number of occurrences of a element in a sorted array.
18. Design a C++ program to find the number of 0s and 1s in a binary array.
19. Design a C++ program to sort the elements and implement binary search.
20. Design a C++ program to find the difference of elements in an array.
21. Design a C++ program to find the product of elements in an array.
22. Design a C++ program to find the standard deviation of elements in an array.
23. Design a C++ program to sort the elements in an array and find the median of the array.
24. Design a C++ Program to find the union of two arrays
25. Design a C++ Program to find the intersection of two arrays
26. Design a C++ program to implement tic tac toe game using arrays.
27. Design a C program to print even numbers in an array.
28. Design a C++ program to print odd numbers in an array.
29. Design a C program to read and print array elements.
30. Design a C++ program to print the Fibonacci series.

31. Design a C++ program to delete an array element.
32. Design a C++ program to insert an element at a given position in an array.

Note: Implement the above programs using dynamic arrays.

33. Design a C++ program to declare a class student with data members SRN, Name, Marks. Write appropriate functions to read and print the data members. Implement the above program using pointers.
34. Design a C++ program to declare a class employee with Emp_id, Name, Salary, Dept. Write appropriate functions to read the data members, compute the gross salary given the DA, HRA, CC, Basic and print the same. Implement the same using pointers.
35. Design a C++ program to declare a class student with data members SRN, Name, Marks. Write appropriate functions to read the data members, compute the grade and percentage of marks and print the result. Implement the above program using pointers.Design a C++ program to declare a structure COMPLEX with data members imag and real. Write appropriate functions to read complex number, compute sum, difference of complex numbers and print the same.

CHAPTER - 3

Chapter 3

Singly Linked List

Introduction

The arrays are static data structures and have a few disadvantages, while they are useful in some ways too. The disadvantages of using arrays can be overcome using the data structure linked list. Linked list finds their applications in real-time like image viewer, web pages, music player, and many more. Hence it is very much necessary to know this linked list data structure. In this chapter, we will be discussing about the linked list types, implementation of the two types of linked list, singly and circular singly linked list.

Structure

This chapter covers the following topics:

- Linked lists
- Singly linked list
    - SLL without header
    - CSLL without header
    - CSLL with a header with detailed operations

Objectives:

After reading this chapter, the reader will know about the disadvantages and advantages of using arrays and how the disadvantages of using arrays will be overcome using linked lists will be known. The types of linked lists and implementation of various operations of singly linked lists and circular singly lists are discussed in detail in this chapter. This chapter will help the reader in writing efficient programs.

3.1 Advantages and Disadvantages of Arrays:

Before discussing the linked lists, let us discuss the advantages and disadvantages of the arrays and how linked lists will overcome the disadvantages of the arrays.

3.1.1 Advantages of Arrays

The advantages of using arrays are as discussed below:

- **Optimization of code:** An array allows storing and accessing a large number of values by writing a small piece of code, thereby optimizing the code.
- **Functionality:** Arrays are one of the most basic data structures to implement most of the data structures and various searching, sorting, and other algorithms. Many large programs can be implemented using an array data structure.
- **Index-based:** Arrays use an index-based data structure, which helps to identify each of the elements in an array easily using the index.
- **Multi-dimensional:** Complex data structures can be implemented using 2-D arrays.
- **Memory allocation:** Arrays store elements in a sequential manner using both static and dynamic allocation techniques.
- **Multiple uses:** The basic data structure of arrays can be used to implement different data structures like stacks, queues, graphs, trees, and more.
- **Faster data access:** Using an array data structure, data accessing is quite easy and fast. Data can be accessed by specifying the array name followed by the index of the array within the [ ] operator.
- **Simple:** Arrays are simple to understand and easy to use.

3.1.2 Disadvantages of Arrays

The disadvantages of using arrays are discussed as follows:

- **Size is fixed:** The size of an array is fixed. The memory allocated to an array cannot be expanded or reduced.
- **Stored contiguously:** Sometimes, enough contiguous memory locations may not be available.
- **Operational limitation:** Deletion and insertion operations, including arrays is a tedious job.

The disadvantages of using arrays can be overcome by using linked lists.

3.2 Linked lists

A linked list is a non-primitive, linear data structure. A linked List is a collection of zero or more nodes where each node has some information. The pictorial representation of a node in the linked list is as shown below:

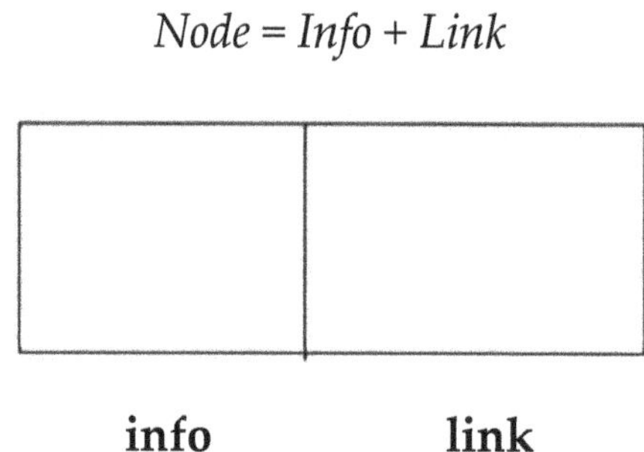

$$Node = Info + Link$$

Fig 3.1: Pictorial representation of a node

A node in a linked list consists of two fields:

- Info field: This field is used to store data or information to be manipulated.
- Link field: The link field contains address of the next node.

3.3 Types of linked lists

The linked lists are classified as shown below:

- Singly linked lists
- Doubly linked lists
- Circular singly linked lists
- Circular doubly linked lists

3.3.1 Singly linked lists

A singly linked list is a linked list which consists of a single field called link field which contains the address of the next node and more than one data or information field. Since the linked list contains single link field, the linked list is called singly linked list.

The pictorial representation of singly linked list is shown below:

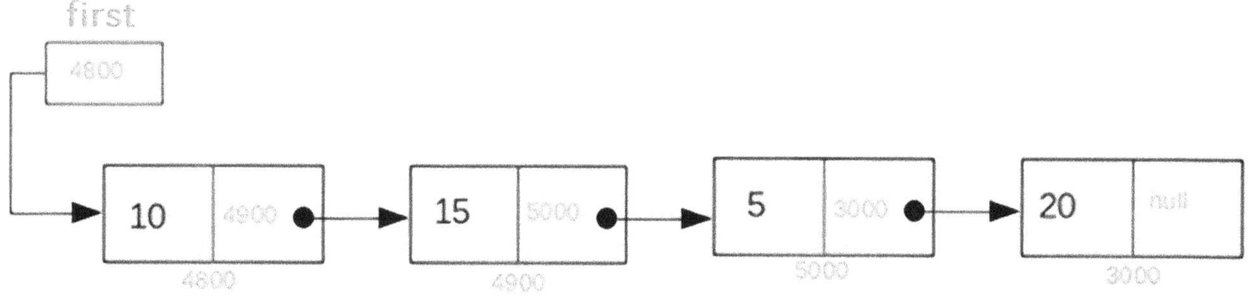

Fig 3.2: Pictorial representation of singly linked list

Observe the following points from the above linked list:

- The list contains 4 nodes and each node consists of two fields info and link.
- The first field of each node contains information or data. The info field can contain any type of data like numbers or character or string.
- The second field that is, the link field of each node contains the address of the next node.
- The link field of last node contains NULL. The NULL field indicates that it is the last node of the list.

3.3.2 Circular singly linked list

A circular singly linked list is a variation of a linked list where the link field of the last node contains the address of the first node.

In a singly linked list, the address of the last node contains NULL, whereas in a circular singly linked list, the link field of the last node contains the address of the first node.

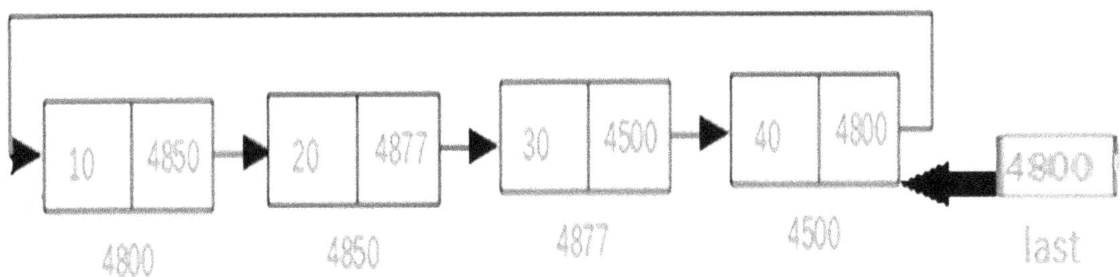

Fig 3.3: Pictorial representation of circular singly linked list

Observe the following points from the above-linked list:

- The list contains 4 nodes, each consisting of two fields: info and link.
- The first field of each node contains information or data. The info field can contain any type of data, like numbers, characters or string.
- The second field, that is, the link field of each node, contains the address of the next node.
- The link field of the last node contains the address of the first node, hence the name circular singly linked list.

3.3.3 Doubly linked list

A doubly linked list is a linear collection of nodes where each node is divided into three nodes:

- info/data: This field contains data or information to be stored.
- llink/prev: This field contains the address of the previous node or the left node
- rlink/next: This field contains the address of the next node or the right node.

rlink and llink are the pointer fields since both the field store the address of the next and previous node respectively.

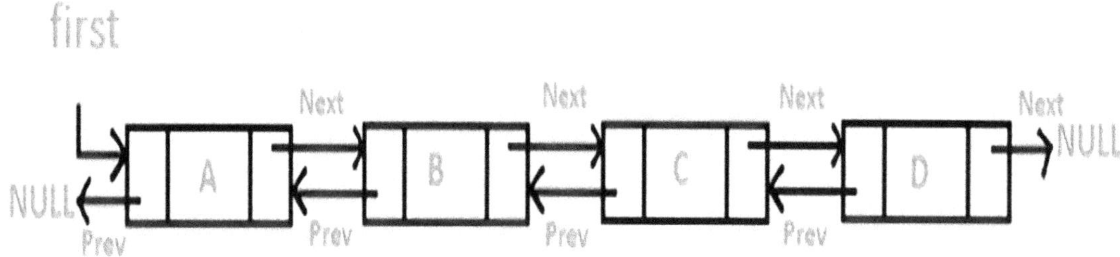

Fig 3.4: Pictorial representation of a doubly linked list

Observe the following points from the above-linked list:

- The list contains four ,nodes and each node consist of three fields: info, llink and rlink.
- The first field that is, llink field of each node contains the address of the previous node.
- The second field of each node contains information or data. The info field can contain any type of, data like numbers or character or string.
- The third field, that is, rlink field of each node contains the address of the next node.
- The rlink field of last node and llink field of first node contains NULL.

3.3.4   Circular doubly linked list

A circular doubly linked list is a variation of doubly linked list where:

- info/data: This field contains data or information to be stored.
- llink/prev: This field contains the address of the previous node or the left node
- rlink/next: This field contains the address of the next node or the right node.

The rlink of the last node contains the address of the first node, and llink of the first node contains address of the last node.

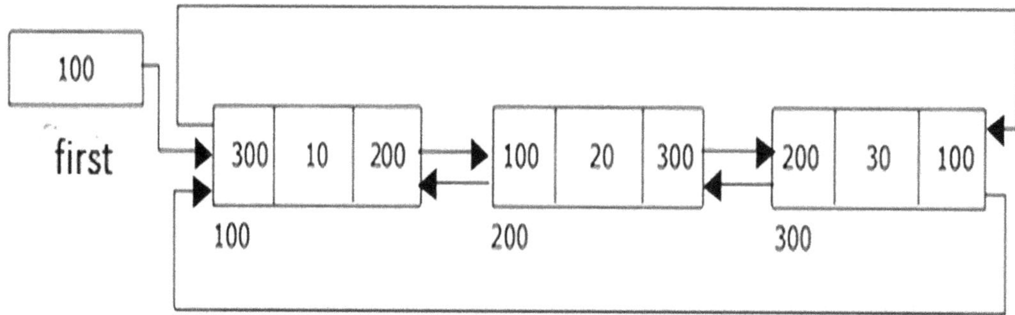

Fig 3.5: Pictorial representation of circular doubly linked list

Observe the following points from the above-linked list:

- The list contains 4 nodes, and each node consists of three fields: info, llink, and rlink.
- The first field that is, llink field of each node contains the address of the previous node.
- The second field of each node contains information or data. The info field can contain any type of data like numbers or characters or strings.
- The third field that is, rlink field of each node contains the address of the next node.

The rlink of the last node contains the address of the first node and llink of the first node contains address of the last node.

3.4 Defining a node in a C++ language

Since the node contains two fields, info and link, and both the fields are of different datatype, the syntax to define a node is shown below:

```
class Node
{
     datatype info;
Node *link;
};
```

Here:

- the info field can be of any of the basic datatypes.
- link field is a pointer variable of the type Node.

3.4.1 Defining a Constructor and a node

The definition of a node and a constructor in a singly linked list is as shown:

```
class Node
{
     public:
     int info;
     Node *link;

     public:
          Node(int value)
          {
                info=value;
                link=NULL;
          }
};
```

```
typedef Node * NODE;
```

A pointer variable head can be declared as shown below:

```
NODE head;
```

3.5   Operations on singly linked lists without header node

The operations that can be performed on singly linked lists are:

- Inserting a node into the list
- Deleting a node from the list
- Traversing a linked list

3.5.1   Insert a node at the front end

Let us consider a list with 4 nodes. Here pointer head contains the address of first node of the list and let us insert a node at the front end of the list:

The sequence of steps to be followed to insert a node at the front end are shown below:

1. Create a new node. Here the name of our node is newnode:

    ```
    NODE newnode=new Node(ele);
    ```

2. Attach pointer head to the link field of newnode:

    ```
    newnode→link=head;
    ```

3. Now newnode has been inserted and always return the address of the newnode

    ```
    return newnode;
    ```

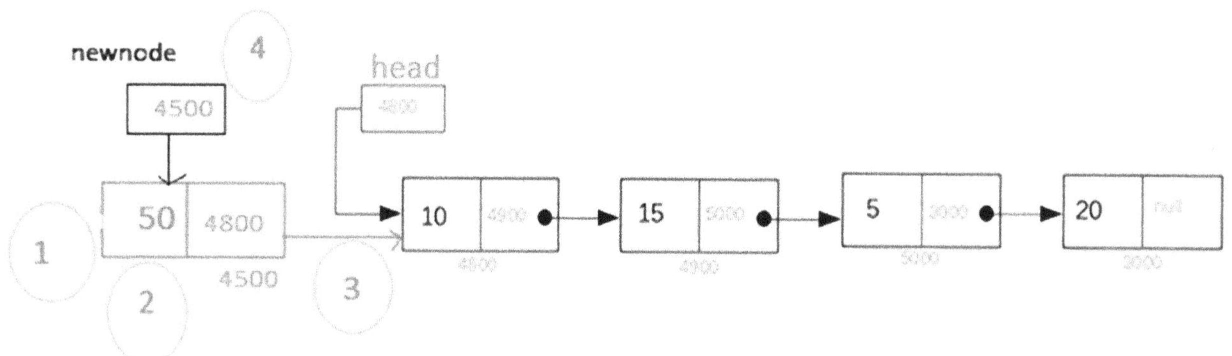

Fig 3.6: To insert an element at the front end of the singly linked list

```
//C++ function to insert an element at the front end of the list:
NODE insert_front(int ele, NODE head)
{
    NODE newnode = new Node(ele);
    newnode→link=head;
    return newnode;
}
```

3.5.2   Insert a node at the rear end

Let us consider a list with 4 nodes. Here pointer **head** contains the address of first node of the list. Let us create a node at the rear end of the list

The sequence of steps to be followed to insert a node at the rear end are shown below:

1.   Create a new node. Here the name of our node is newnode:

```
NODE newnode = new Node(ele);
```

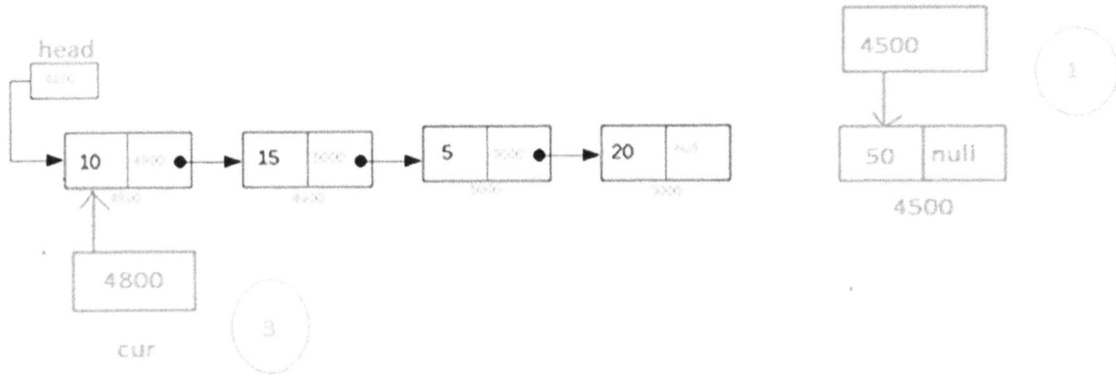

Fig 3.7: To insert an element at the front end of the singly linked list

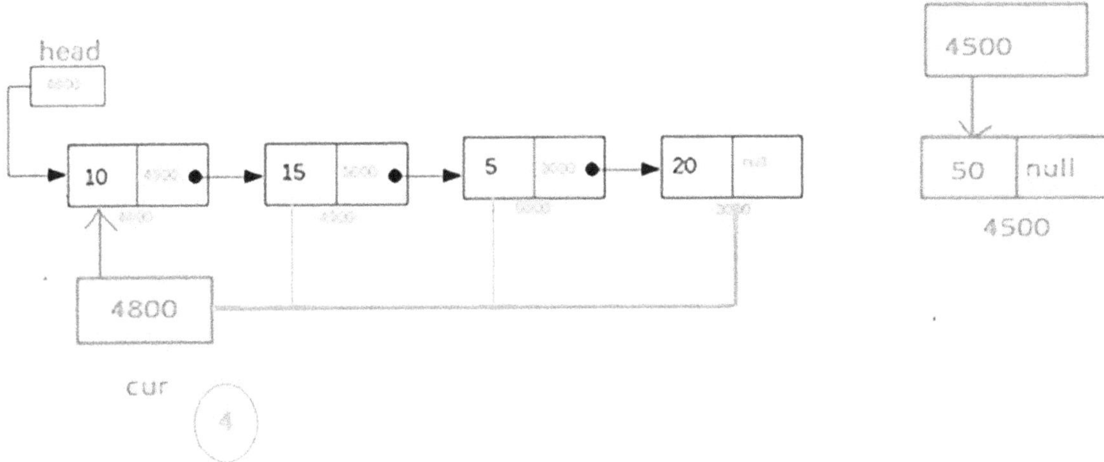

Fig 3.8: To insert an element at the front end of the singly linked list

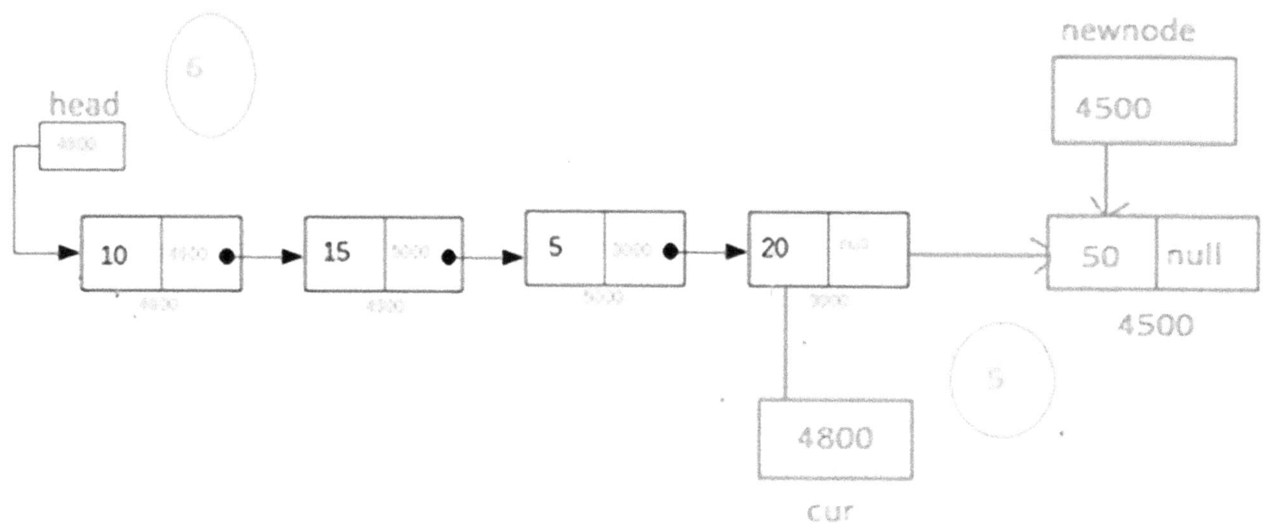

Fig 3.9: To insert an element at the rear end of the singly linked list

If a node newnode is inserted for the first time, then newnode is the first node.

```
if (head==NULL)
{
        head=newnode;
        return head;
}
```

If the list is not empty, then traverse till the end of the list and try to find the last node of the list. To do that we use a pointer cur which initially points to the first node.

```
cur = head;
```

Now to obtain the address of the last node traverse through the list till cur reaches the last node.

```
while (cur→link≠NULL)
        cur=cur→link;
```

Insert newnode to the end of the list.

```
cur→link=newnode;
```

```
//C++ function to insert an element at the rear end of the list:
NODE insert_rear(int ele, NODE head)
{
    NODE cur;
    NODE newnode = new Node(ele);
    if (head==NULL)
```

```
    {
        head=newnode;
        return head;
    }
    cur=head;
while (cur→link≠NULL)
    {
            cur=cur→link;
    }
    cur→link=newnode;
    return head;
}
```

3.5.3   Delete a node at the front end

The various steps to be followed to delete a node from front end are:

A temporary variable called temp to be pointed to the head node:

```
temp = head;
```

Update pointer temp to point to the second node in the list:

```
temp=temp→link;
```

Delete the head node:

```
delete head;
```

Return the first node called temp to the calling function:

```
return temp;
```

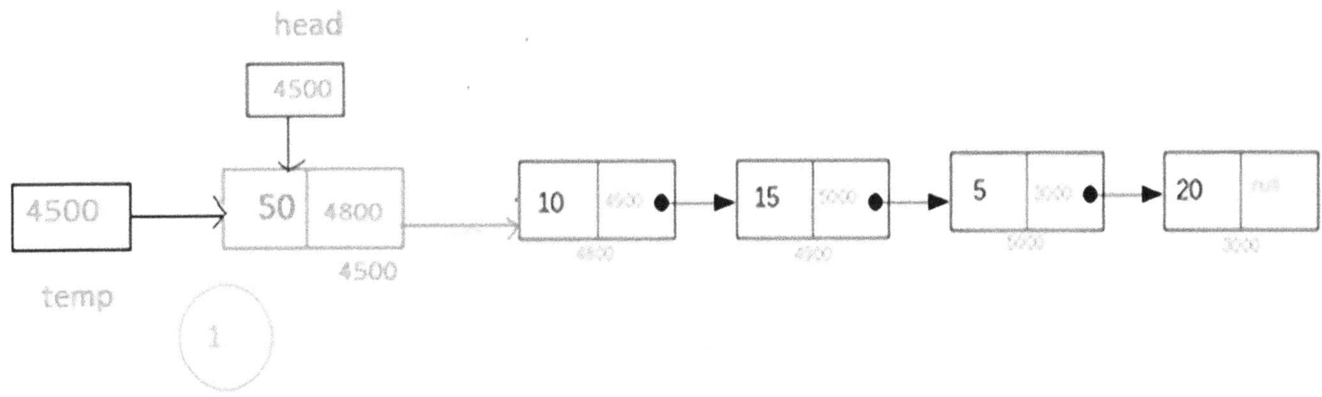

Fig 3.10: To delete an element from the front end of the singly linked list

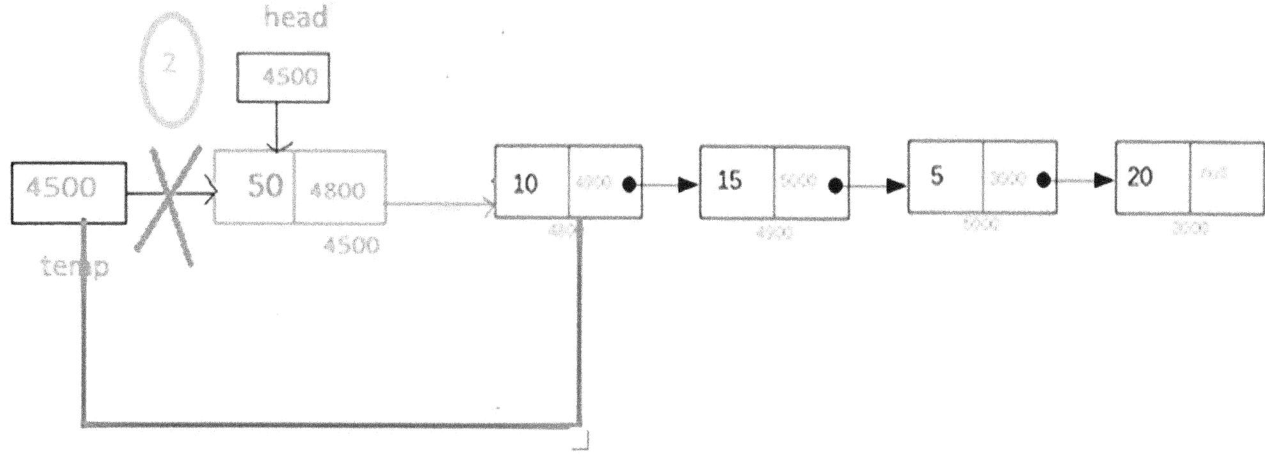

Fig 3.11: To delete an element from the front end of the singly linked list

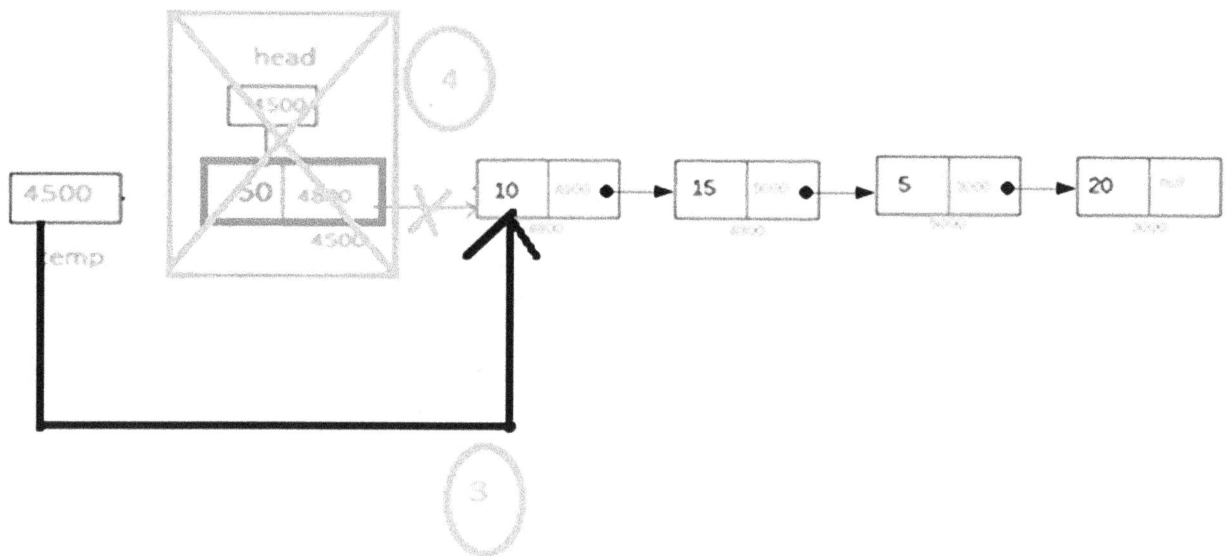

Fig 3.12: To delete an element from the front end of the singly linked list

```cpp
// C++ function to delete an element from the front end:
NODE delete_front(NODE head)
{
    NODE temp;
    if(head==NULL)
    {
        cout<<"Cannot delete as list is empty"<<endl;
        return NULL;
    }
    temp=head;
    temp=temp→link;
```

```
        cout<<"element deleted is"<<head→info<<endl;
        delete head;
        return temp;
}
```

3.5.4 Delete a node from the rear end

The various steps to be followed to delete a node from rear end are:

1. If list is empty, it is not possible to delete any element from an empty list:

```
if (head == NULL)
{
        cout<<"list is empty, cannot delete\n";
        return NULL;
}
```

2. Consider a list that contains a single node. After deletion, the list should be empty.

```
if (head→link==NULL)
{
        cout<<"deleted element is"<<head→info<<endl;
        delete head;
        return NULL;
}
```

3. When list has more than one node, to delete the last node it is necessary to find the last node and its previous node. To do this, we use two pointers cur and prev.

We initialize cur to the first node and prev to NULL. We go on traversing through the list until cur points to the last node and prev to its previous node.

This can be achieved by the following set of statements:

```
prev = NULL;
cur = head;
while(cur→link≠ NULL)
{
        prev=cur;
        cur=cur→link;
}
cout<<"deleted element is"<<cur→info<<endl;
```

4. Delete the last node:

```
delete cur;
```

5. Assign prev ->link to NULL, as now prev is the last node of the list:

```
prev→link=NULL;
```

6. Return the head node.

```
return head;
```

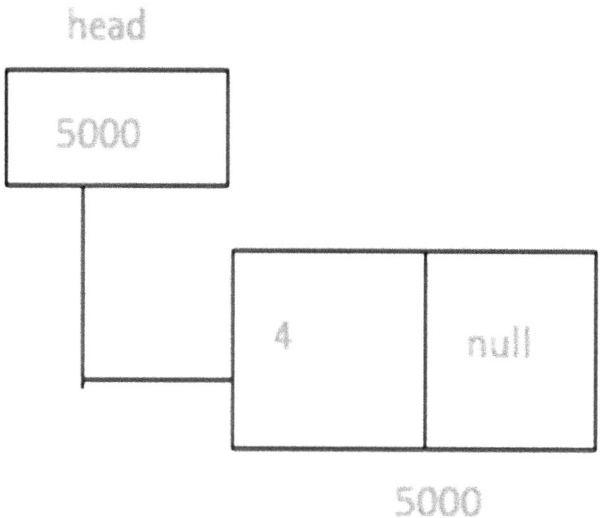

Fig 3.13: *To delete an element from the rear end of the singly linked list*

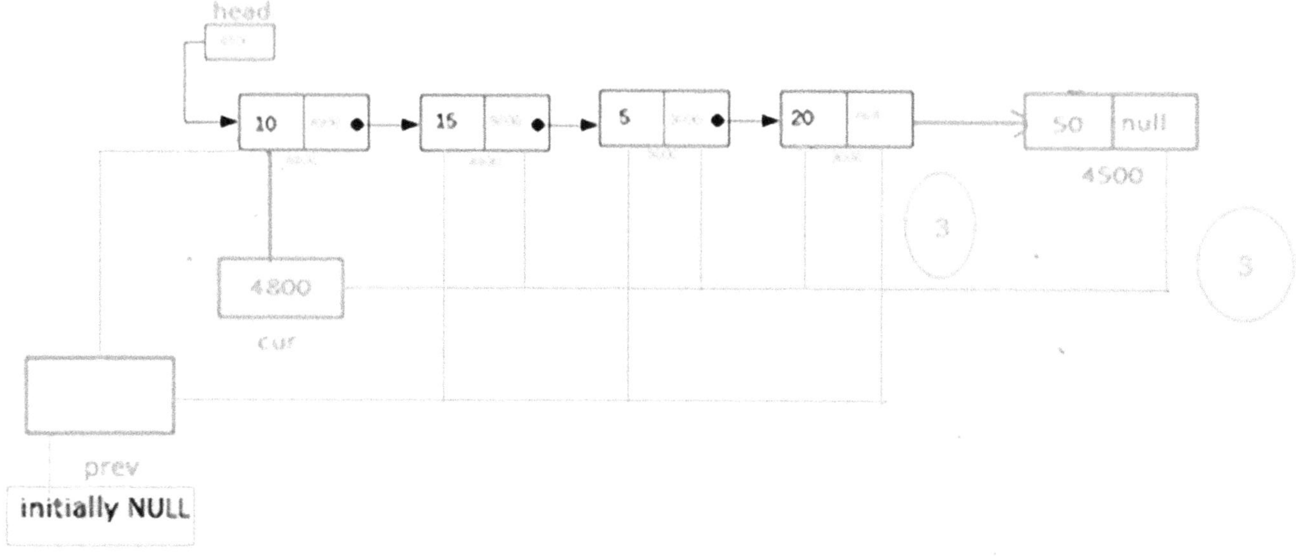

Fig 3.14: *To delete an element from the rear end of the singly linked list*

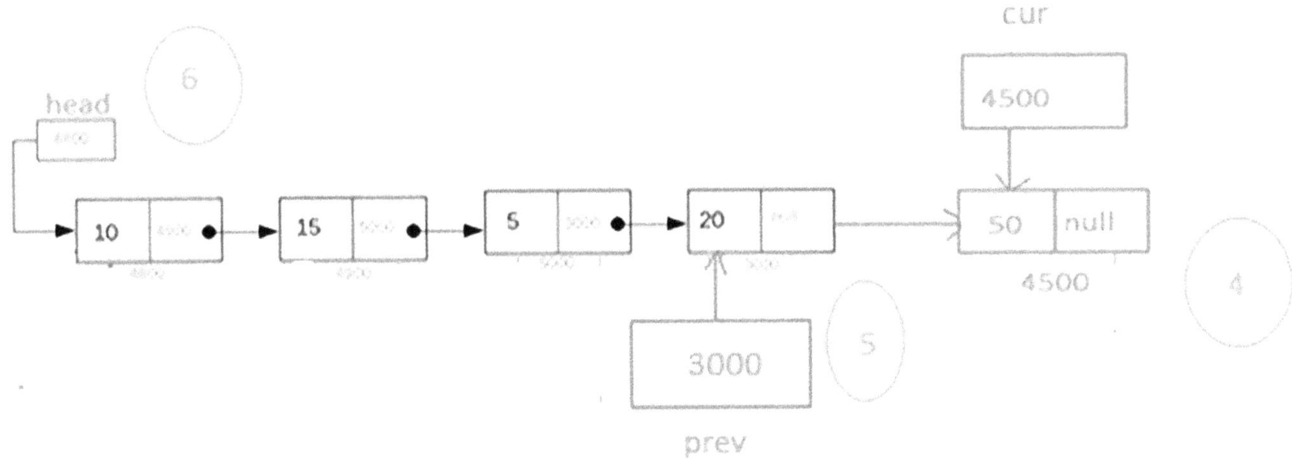

Fig 3.15: To delete an element from the rear end of the singly linked list

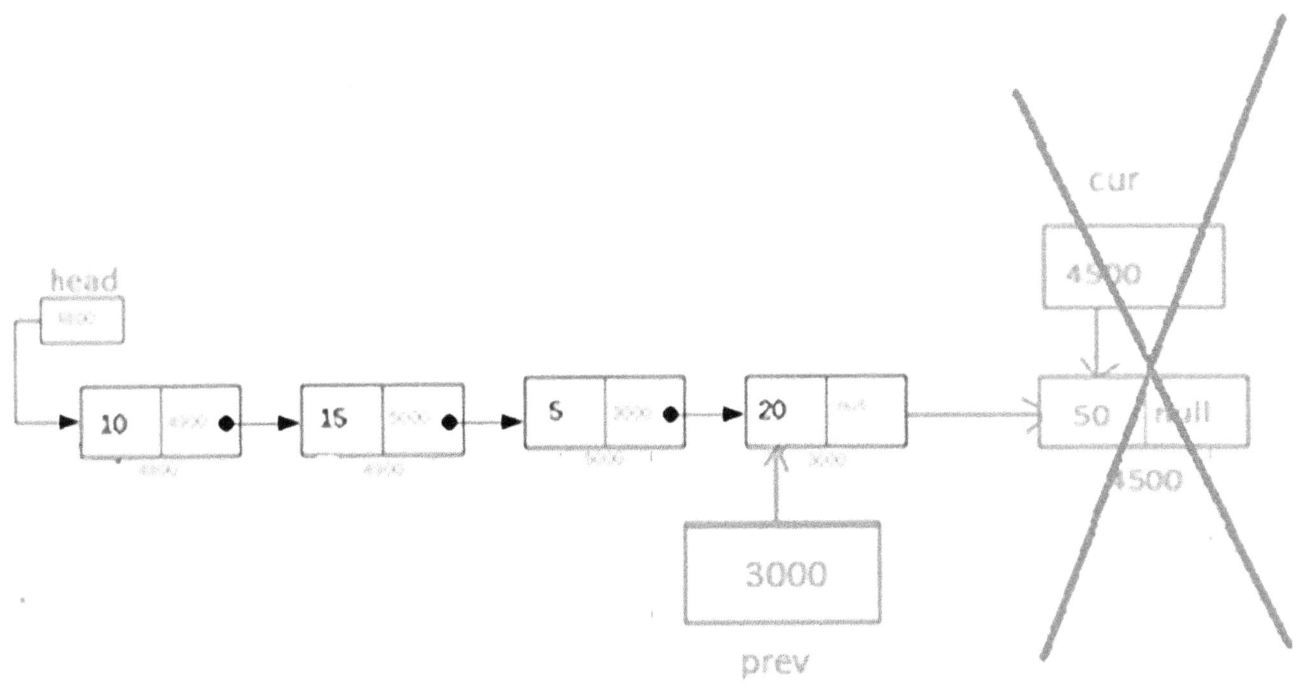

Fig 3.16: To delete an element from the rear end of the singly linked list

```cpp
// C++ function to delete an element from the rear end:
NODE delete_rear(NODE head)
{
    NODE cur,prev;
    if (head == NULL)
```

```cpp
{
        cout<<"list is empty, cannot delete\n";
        return NULL;
}
if (head→link==NULL)
{
        cout<<"deleted element is"<<head→info<<endl;
        delete head;
        return NULL;
}
prev = NULL;
cur = head;
while(cur→link≠ NULL)
{
        prev=cur;
        cur=cur→link;
}
cout<<"deleted element is"<<cur→info<<endl;
delete cur;
prev→link=NULL;
return head;
}
```

3.5.5   Display the elements of the singly linked list

The various steps to be followed to display the nodes of Singly Linked List are:

1. If list is empty, it is not possible to display elements of an empty list:

```cpp
if (head == NULL)
    {
        cout<<"list is empty, no elements to display"<<endl;
        return;
    }
```

2. To display the elements of list, initialize temp to head:

```cpp
temp=head;
```

3. Traverse through the list, and print the info field until the end of the list is reached:

```cpp
while(temp≠NULL)
```

```
    {
        cout<<temp→info<<endl;
        temp=temp→link;
    }
```

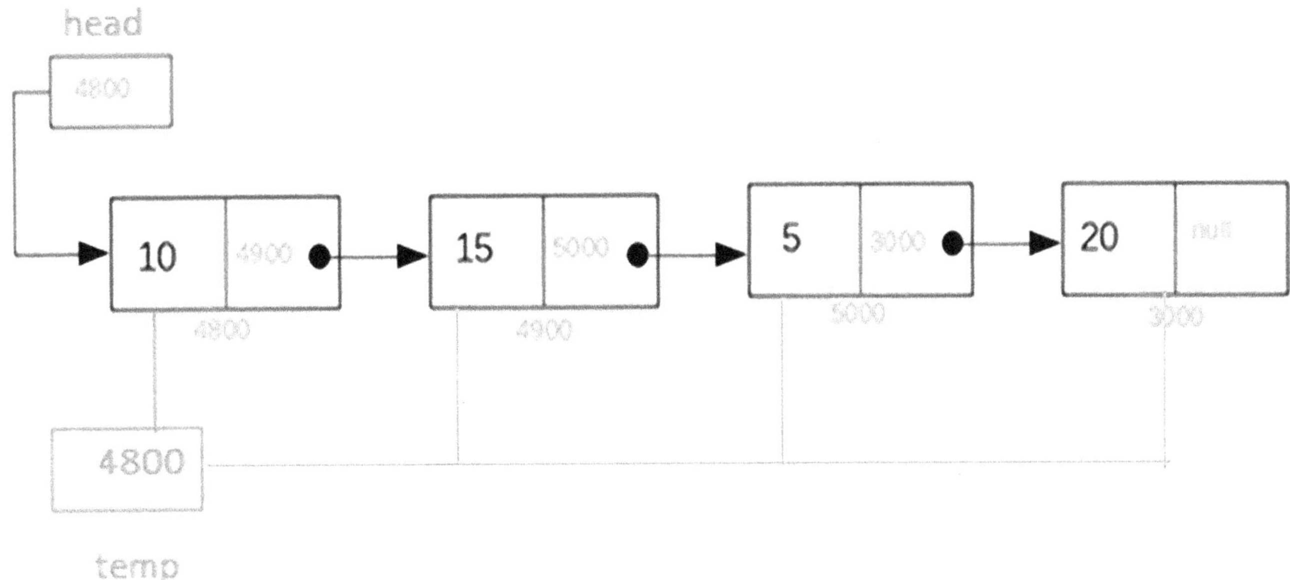

Fig 3.17: To display the elements of the singly linked list

```
// C++ function to display elements of Singly Linked List:
void display(NODE head)
{
    NODE temp;
    if (head == NULL)
    {
        cout<<"list is empty, no elements to display"<<endl;
        return;
    }
    temp=head;
    while(temp≠NULL)
    {
        cout<<temp→info<<endl;
        temp=temp→link;
    }
}
```

3.5.6   Search for an element in the singly linked list

The various steps to be followed to search for an element in Singly Linked List are:

1. If list is empty, it is not possible to display elements of an empty list

```
if (head == NULL)
{
      cout<<"list is empty, no elements to search\n"<<endl;

      return;

}
```

2. To search for an element in SLL, traverse till the end of list and compare key with the info field. If key is found, print key found else key not found:

```
cur=head;
while (cur≠ NULL)
{
      if(key==cur→info)
      {
          break;
      }
      cur=cur→link;
}
```

```
//C++ function to search for an element in the singly linked list:
void search(NODE head, int key)
{
      NODE cur;
      if (head == NULL)
      {
          cout<<"list is empty, no elements to search\n"<<endl;
          return;
      }
      cur=head;
      while (cur≠ NULL)
      {
          if(key==cur→info)
          {
              break;
          }
```

```
        cur=cur→link;
    }
    if(cur==NULL)
    {
        cout<<"key Not Found\n"<<endl;
        return;
    }
    cout<<"Key Found\n"<<endl;
}
```

3.5.7 Insert a node before the given key element

The various steps to be followed to insert a node before the given key element:

1. Create a new node named newnode.

```
        NODE newnode = new Node(ele);
```

2. List is empty.

If list is empty, there are no nodes to compare with the key element. Just print the message list is empty.

```
    if(head==NULL)
    {
        cout<<"List empty, cannot insert element"<<endl;
        return NULL;
    }
```

If list is not empty and cur->info==key, we use two pointers cur and prev.

We initialize cur to head node and prev to NULL. We go on traversing through the list until

```
    cur→info = key
    while(cur→link≠NULL)
    {
        if(cur→info==key)
        {
            newnode→link=cur;
            prev→link=newnode;
        }
        prev=cur;
        cur=cur→link;
    }
```

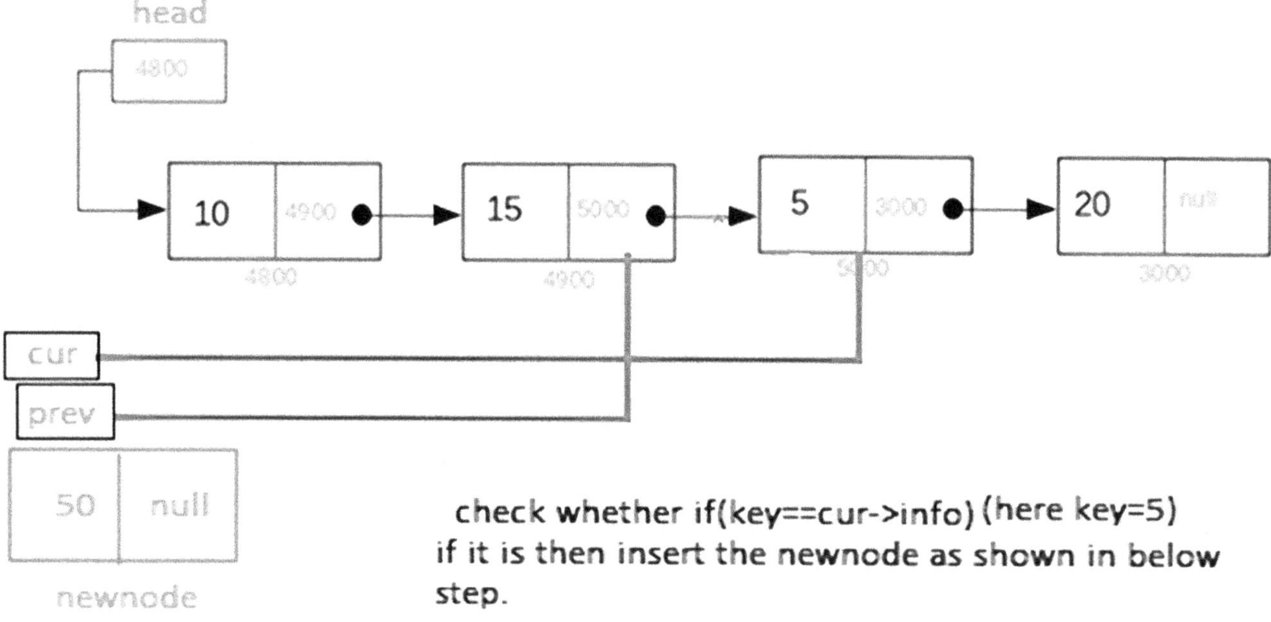

Fig 3.18: Insert a node before the given key element

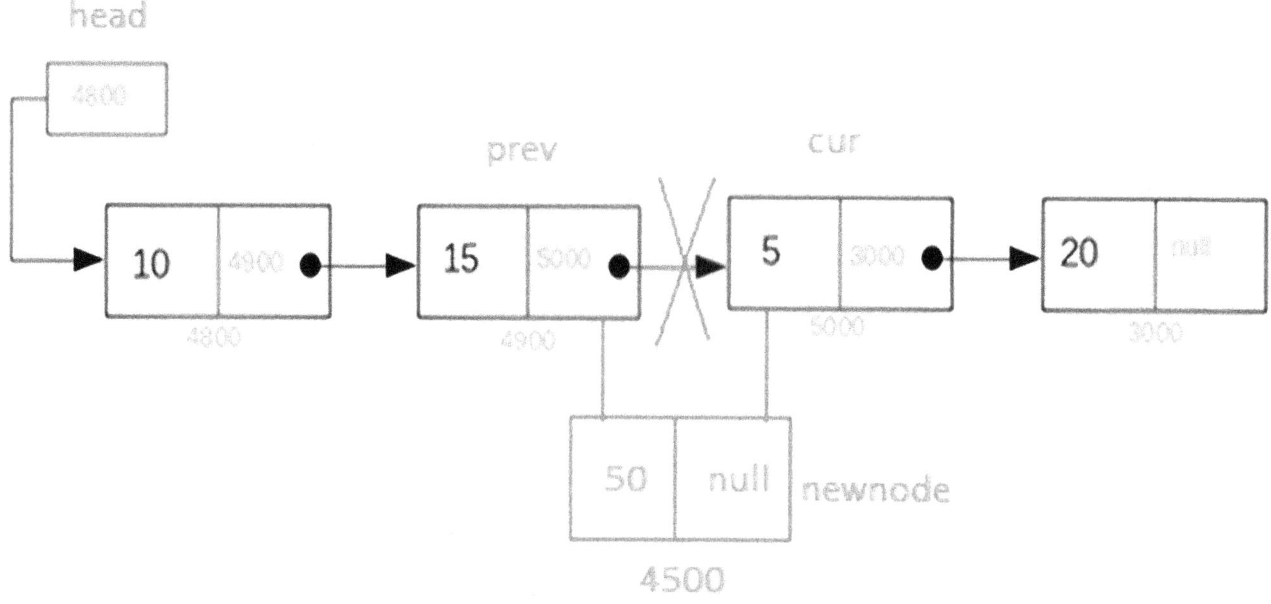

Fig 3.19: Insert a node before the given key element

```cpp
//C++ function to insert a node before the given key element:
NODE add_bef_key(int ele,int key,NODE head)
{

      NODE cur,prev;
      NODE newnode = new Node(ele);

      if(head==NULL)
      {
            cout<<"List empty, cannot insert element"<<endl;
            return NULL;
      }

      prev=NULL;
      cur=head;

      while(cur→link≠NULL)
      {

            if(cur→info==key)
            {
                  newnode→link=cur;
                  prev→link=newnode;
            }
            prev=cur;
            cur=cur→link;
      }
      if(cur→link==NULL)
   {
      cout<<"key not found"<<endl;
   }
   return head;
}
```

3.5.8   Insert a node after the given key element

The various steps to be followed to insert a node after the given key element:

1. Create a new node named newnode.

```cpp
          NODE newnode = new Node(ele);                    }
```

2. List is empty.

If list is empty, there are no nodes to compare with the key element, just print the message list is empty.

```
if(head==NULL)
{
        cout<<"List empty, cannot insert element"<<endl;
        return NULL;
}
```

If list is not empty and cur->info==key, we use two pointers cur.

We initialize cur to head. We go on traversing through the list until cur.info = key

```
while(cur→link ≠NULL)
{
        if(cur→info==key)
        {
                newnode→link=cur→link;
                cur→link=newnode;
        }
        cur=cur→link;
}
```

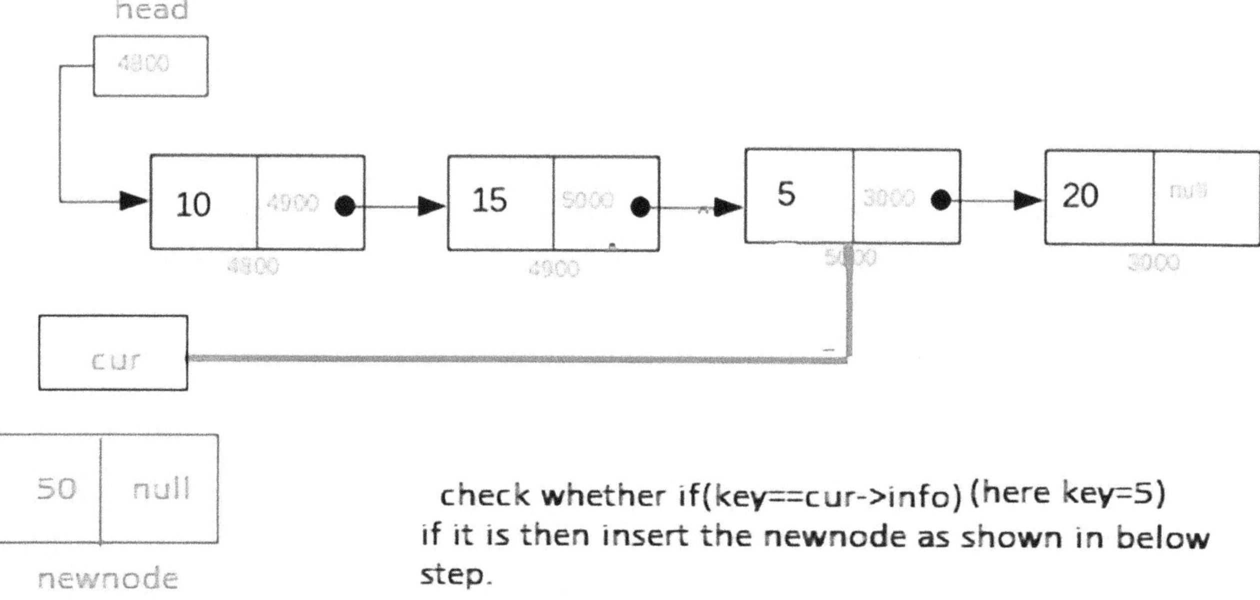

Fig 3.20: Insert a node after the given key element

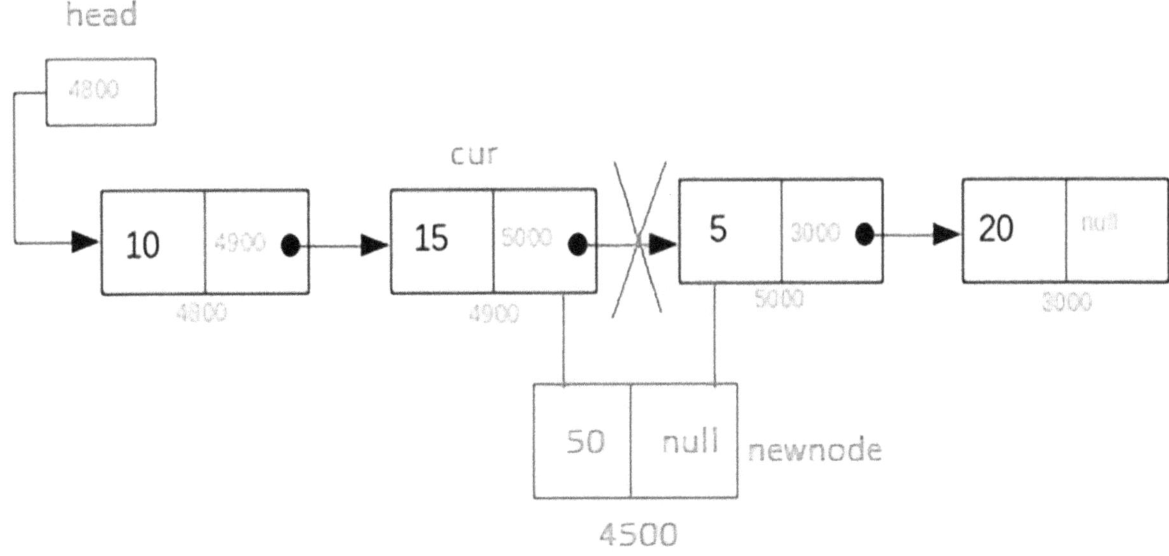

Fig 3.21: *Insert a node after the given key element*

```cpp
//C++ function to insert a node after the given key element:
NODE add_after_key(int ele, int key, NODE head)
{
    NODE cur;

    NODE newnode = new Node(ele);

    if(head==NULL)
    {
        cout<<"List empty, cannot insert element"<<endl;
        return NULL;
    }

    cur=head;

    while(cur→link ≠NULL)
    {
        if(cur→info==key)
        {
            newnode→link=cur→link;
            cur→link=newnode;
        }
        cur=cur→link;
    }
```

```cpp
    if(cur→link==NULL)
    {
        cout<<"key not found"<<endl;
    }
    return head;
}
```

3.6 C++ Program to implement the operations of singly linked list without header

```cpp
#include<iostream>
using namespace std;

class Node
{
    public:
    int info;
    Node *link;

    public:
        Node(int value)
        {
                info=value;
                link=NULL;
        }
};


typedef Node* NODE;


//C++ function to insert an element at the front end of the list:
NODE insert_front(int ele, NODE head)
{
    NODE newnode = new Node(ele);
    newnode→link=head;
    return newnode;
}


//C++ function to insert an element at the rear end of the list:
NODE insert_rear(int ele, NODE head)
{
    NODE cur;
    NODE newnode = new Node(ele);
```

```cpp
    if (head==NULL)
    {
     head=newnode;
          return head;
    }
    cur=head;
  while (cur→link≠NULL)
    {
          cur=cur→link;
    }
    cur→link=newnode;
  return head;
}


// C++ function to delete an element from the front end:
NODE delete_front(NODE head)
{
    NODE temp;

    if(head==NULL)
    {
        cout<<"Cannot delete as list is empty"<<endl;;
        return NULL;
    }

    temp=head;
    temp=temp→link;

    cout<<"element deleted is"<<head→info<<endl;

    delete head;
    return temp;
}


// C++ function to delete an element from the rear end:
NODE delete_rear(NODE head)
{
    NODE cur,prev;
    if (head == NULL)
    {
        cout<<"list is empty, cannot delete\n";
        return NULL;
    }
```

```cpp
    if (head→link==NULL)
    {
            cout<<"deleted element is"<<head→info<<endl;
            delete head;
            return NULL;
    }
    prev = NULL;
    cur = head;
    while(cur→link≠ NULL)
    {
            prev=cur;
            cur=cur→link;
    }
    cout<<"deleted element is"<<cur→info<<endl;
    delete cur;
    prev→link=NULL;
    return head;
}


// C++ function to display elements of Singly Linked List:
void display(NODE head)
{
    NODE temp;
    if (head == NULL)
    {
            cout<<"list is empty, no elements to display"<<endl;
            return;
    }
    temp=head;
    while(temp≠NULL)
    {
            cout<<temp→info<<endl;
            temp=temp→link;
    }
}


//C++ function to search for an element in the singly linked list:
void search(NODE head, int key)
{
    NODE cur;
    if (head == NULL)
```

```cpp
{
        cout<<"list is empty, no elements to search\n"<<endl;
        return;
    }
    cur=head;
    while (cur≠ NULL)
    {
        if(key==cur→info)
        {
            break;
        }
        cur=cur→link;
    }
    if(cur==NULL)
    {
        cout<<"key Not Found\n"<<endl;
        return;
    }
    cout<<"Key Found\n"<<endl;
}


//C++ function to insert a node before the given key element:

NODE add_bef_key(int ele,int key,NODE head)
{

    NODE cur,prev;

    NODE newnode = new Node(ele);

    newnode→info=ele;
    newnode→link=NULL;

    if(head==NULL)
    {
        cout<<"List empty, cannot insert element"<<endl;
        return NULL;
    }

    prev=NULL;
    cur=head;
```

```cpp
    while(cur→link≠NULL)
    {

        if(cur→info==key)
        {
            newnode→link=cur;
            prev→link=newnode;
        }
        prev=cur;
        cur=cur→link;
    }
    if(cur→link==NULL)
{

    cout<<"key not found"<<endl;

}
    return head;
}


//C++ function to insert a node after the given key element:
NODE add_after_key(int ele, int key, NODE head)
{
    NODE cur;

    NODE newnode = new Node(ele);
    newnode→info=ele;
    newnode→link=NULL;

    if(head==NULL)
    {
        cout<<"List empty, cannot insert element"<<endl;
        return NULL;
    }

    cur=head;

    while(cur→link ≠NULL)
    {
        if(cur→info==key)
        {
            newnode→link=cur→link;
            cur→link=newnode;
        }
```

```cpp
                cur=cur→link;
        }
        if(cur→link==NULL)
        {
                cout<<"key not found"<<endl;
        }
        return head;
}


//Main function

int main()
{
        NODE head;
        head=NULL;
        int ele,key,choice;
        for(;;)
        {
                cout<<"1.Display the contents"<<endl<<
                        "2.Add  at the beginning"<<endl<<
                        "3.Add at the end"<<endl<<
                        "4.Delete_front"<<endl<<
                        "5.Delete_rear"<<endl<<
                        "6.Search"<<endl<<
                        "7.Add after key"<<endl<<
                        "8.Add before key"<<endl<<
                        "9.Exit."<<endl;
                cout<<"Enter your choice: "<<endl;
                cin>>choice;
                switch(choice)
                {
                        case 1:
                                display(head);
                                break;
                        case 2:
                                cout<<"enter the element to be inserted"<<endl;
                                cin>>ele;
                                head=insert_front(ele,head);
                                break;
                        case 3:
                                cout<<"enter the element to be inserted"<<endl;
                                cin>>ele;
```

```cpp
                        head=insert_rear(ele,head);
                        break;
                case 4:
                        head=delete_front(head);
                        break;
                case 5:
                        head=delete_rear(head);
                        break;
                case 6:
                        cout<<"enter the key to be searched"<<endl;
                        cin>>key;
                        search(head,key);
                        break;
                case 7:
                        cout<<"enter the element to be inserted"<<endl;
                        cin>>ele;
                        cout<<"enter the key"<<endl;
                        cin>>key;
                        head=add_after_key(ele,key,head);
                        break;
                case 8:
                        cout<<"enter the element to be inserted"<<endl;
                        cin>>ele;
                        cout<<"enter the key"<<endl;
                        cin>>key;
                        head=add_bef_key(ele,key,head);
                        break;
                default:
                        printf("invalid choice");

            }
        }
        return 0;
}
```

Output:

1.Display the contents

2.Add at the beginning

3.Add at the end

4. Delete_front

```
5.Delete_rear
6.Search
7.Add after key
8. Add before key
9.Exit.
Enter your choice:
2
enter the element to be inserted
10
1.Display the contents
2.Add  at the beginning
3.Add at the end
4. Delete_front
5.Delete_rear
6.Search
7.Add after key
8. Add before key
9.Exit.
Enter your choice:
3
enter the element to be inserted
20
1.Display the contents
2.Add  at the beginning
3.Add at the end
4. Delete_front
5.Delete_rear
6.Search
7.Add after key
8. Add before key
9.Exit.
Enter your choice:
7
enter the element to be inserted
15
enter the key
10
```

```
key not found
1.Display the contents
2.Add  at the beginning
3.Add at the end
4. Delete_front
5.Delete_rear
6.Search
7.Add after key
8. Add before key
9.Exit.
Enter your choice:
8
enter the element to be inserted
12
enter the key
15
key not found
1.Display the contents
2.Add  at the beginning
3.Add at the end
4. Delete_front
5.Delete_rear
6.Search
7.Add after key
8. Add before key
9.Exit.
Enter your choice:
1
10
12
15
20
1.Display the contents
2.Add  at the beginning
3.Add at the end
4. Delete_front
5.Delete_rear
```

```
6.Search
7.Add after key
8. Add before key
9.Exit.
Enter your choice:
6
enter the key to be searched
15
Key Found
1.Display the contents
2.Add  at the beginning
3.Add at the end
4. Delete_front
5.Delete_rear
6.Search
7.Add after key
8. Add before key
9.Exit.
Enter your choice:
4
element deleted is10
1.Display the contents
2.Add  at the beginning
3.Add at the end
4. Delete_front
5.Delete_rear
6.Search
7.Add after key
8. Add before key
9.Exit.
Enter your choice:
5
deleted element is20
1.Display the contents
2.Add  at the beginning
3.Add at the end
4. Delete_front
```

```
5.Delete_rear
6.Search
7.Add after key
8. Add before key
9.Exit.
Enter your choice:
1
12
15
```

3.7 Circular Singly Linked List without Header node

Circular singly linked list is a variation of linked list where link field of last node contains the address of the first node.

In singly linked list, the address of the last node contains NULL whereas in circular singly linked list, the link field of the last node contains address of the first node.

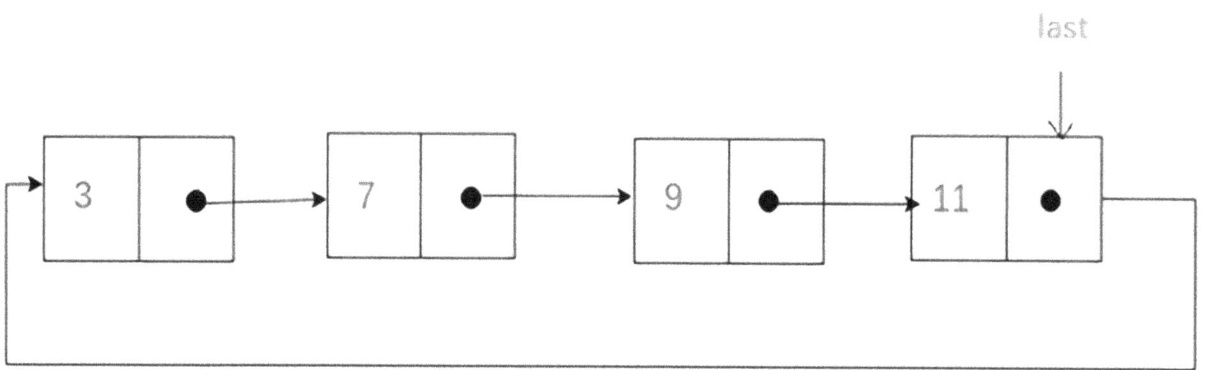

Fig 3.22: Pictorial representation of Circular Singly Linked List

Observe the following points from the above linked list:

- The list contains 4 nodes and each node consists of two fields info and link.
- The first field of each node contains information or data. The info field can contain any type of data like numbers or character or string.
- The second field, that is, link field of each node contains the address of the next node.
- The link field of last node contains address of the first node, hence the name circular singly linked list.

3.8   Operations on Circular Singly Linked Lists

The operations that can be performed on Circular Singly Linked Lists are:

- Inserting a node into the list
- Deleting a node from the list
- Search in a list
- Display the contents of list

3.8.1   Insert a node at the front end

The various steps to be followed to insert a node at the front end:

1. Create a new node named newnode

```
NODE newnode = new Node(ele);
```

2. Establish a link between newnode and the last node.

```
newnode→link = last→link;
```

3. Establish a link between newnode and the last node.

```
last→link=newnode;
```

4. Return the last node

```
return last;
```

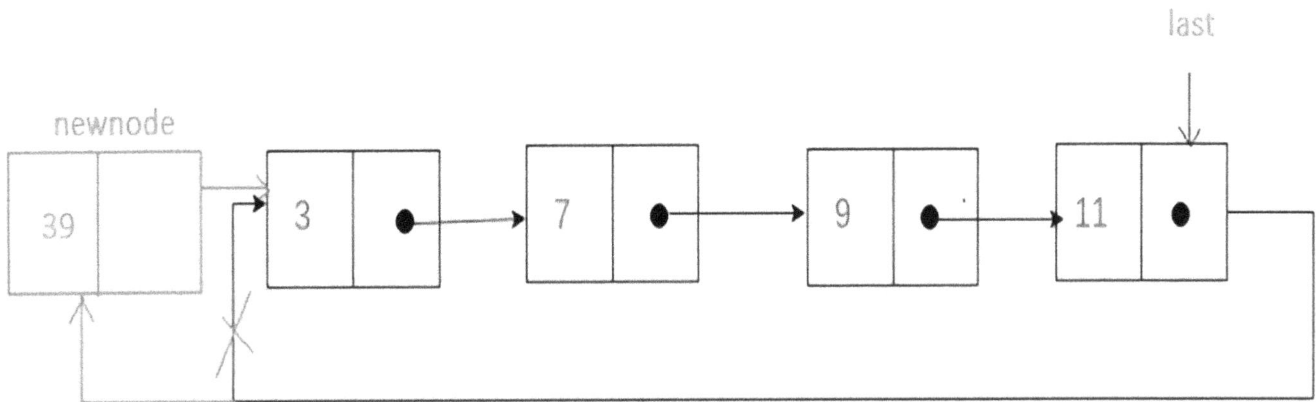

Fig 3.23: Insert a node at the front end

```cpp
//C++ function to insert a node at the front end
NODE insert_front(int ele, NODE last)
{
    NODE newnode = new Node(ele);

    if(last==NULL)
            last=newnode;
    else
    newnode→link = last→link;
    last→link=newnode;
    return last;
}
```

3.8.2 Insert a node at the rear end

The various steps to be followed to insert a node at the rear end:

1. Create a new node named newnode.

```cpp
NODE newnode = new Node(ele);
```

2. Establish a link between first node and link field of last node.

```cpp
newnode→link = last→link;
```

3. Establish a link between last node and newnode.

```cpp
last→link=newnode;
```

4. Return the last node

```cpp
last=newnode;
return last;
```

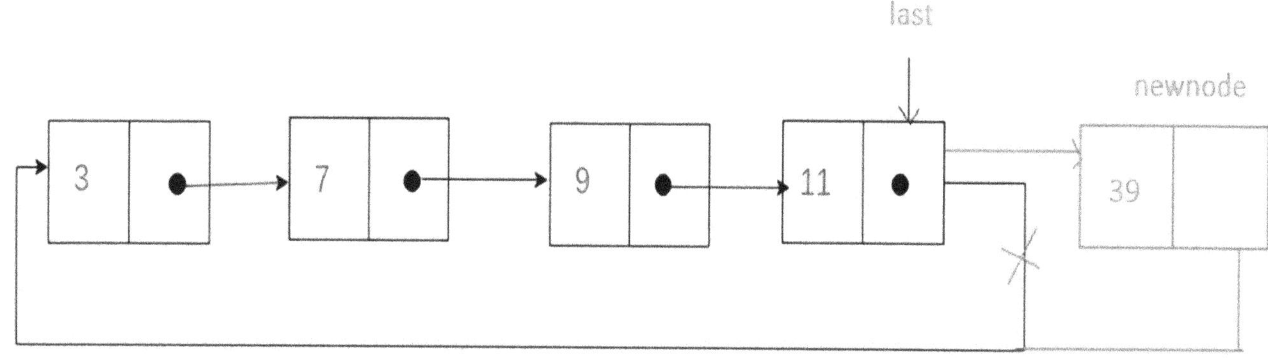

Fig 3.24: Insert a node at the rear end

```
//C++ function to insert a node at the rear end
NODE insert_rear(int ele, NODE last)
{
      NODE newnode = new Node(ele);

      if(last==NULL)
            last=newnode;
      else
      newnode→link = last→link;
      last→link=newnode;
      return newnode;
}
```

3.8.3 Delete a node from the front end

The various steps to be followed to delete a node at the front end:

1. Obtain address of the first node

```
first=last→link;
```

2. Link the last node to the link of the first node

```
last→link=first→link;
```

3. Delete the first node.

```
delete first;
```

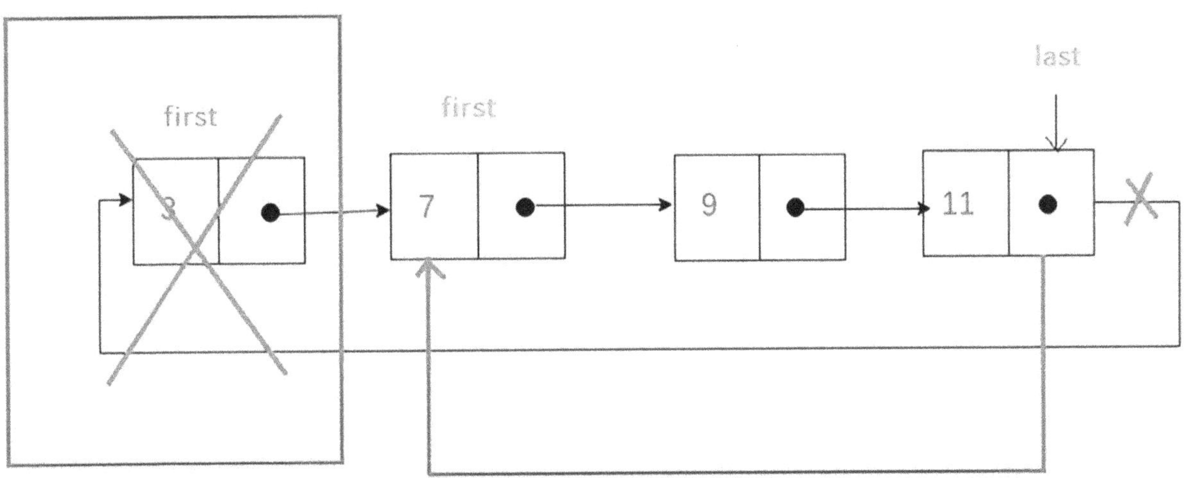

Fig 3.25: Delete a node at the front end

```cpp
//C++ function to delete a node at the front end
NODE delete_front(NODE last)
{
    NODE temp, first;

    if (last == NULL)
    {
        cout<<"List is empty"<<endl;
        return NULL;
    }

    if (last→link==last)
    {
        cout<<"element deleted is"<<last→info<<endl;
        delete last;
        return NULL;
    }

    first=last→link;
    last→link=first→link;

    cout<<"element deleted is"<<first→info;
    delete first;

    return last;
}
```

3.8.4   Delete a node from the rear end

The various steps to be followed to delete a node at the rear end:

1. Obtain the address of predecessor node to last.

```cpp
while(prev→link≠last)
        prev=prev→link;
```

2. Establish the connection between the first node and the prev node.

```cpp
prev→link=last→link;
```

3. Delete the last node

```cpp
delete last;
```

4. Return the address of last node

```
return prev;
```

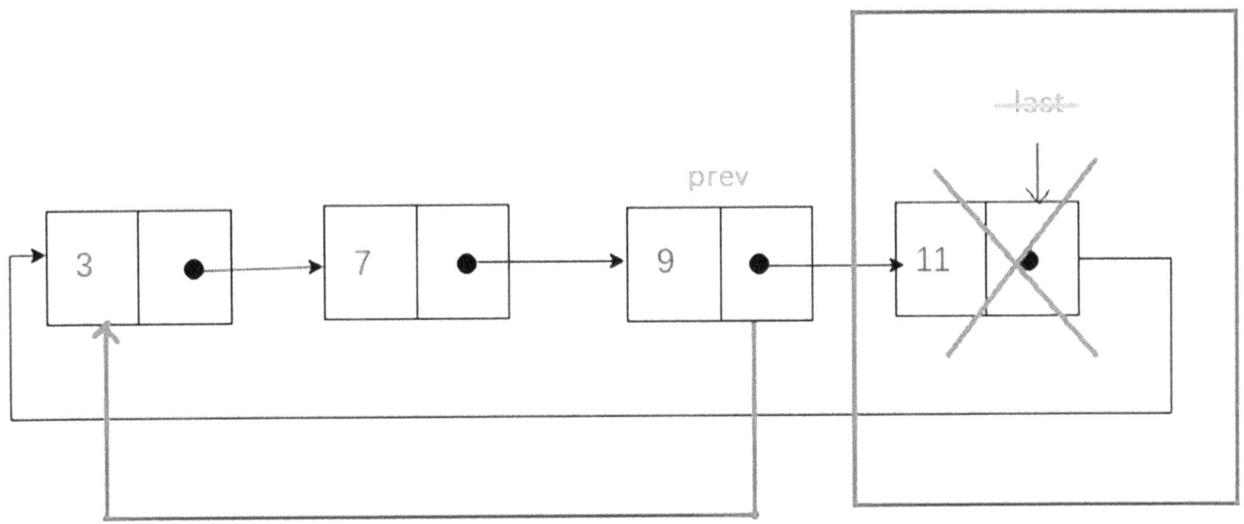

Fig 3.26: *Delete a node from the rear end*

```cpp
//C++ function to delete a node at the rear end
NODE delete_rear (NODE last)
{
    NODE prev;

    if (last == NULL)
    {
        cout<<"List is empty"<<endl;
        return NULL;
    }

    if (last→link==last)
    {
        cout<<"element deleted is"<<last→info<<endl;
        delete last;
        return NULL;
    }
    prev=last→link;
    while(prev→link≠ last)
            prev=prev→link;
    prev→link=last→link;
```

```cpp
        cout<<"element deleted is"<<last->info<<endl;
        delete last;

        return prev;
}
```

3.8.5   Display the elements of Circular Singly Linked List

```cpp
void display(NODE last)
{
        NODE temp;

        if (last == NULL)
        {
                cout<<"List is empty"<<endl;
                return;
        }

        cout<<"Contents of list are"<<endl;
        temp=last->link;

        while (temp!=last)
        {
                cout<<temp->info<<endl;
                temp=temp->link;
        }
        cout<<temp->info<<endl;
}
```

3.9   C++ Program to implement the operations of CSLL without header node

```cpp
#include<iostream>
using namespace std;

//C++ function to insert an element at the front end of the list:
class Node
{
        public:
        int info;
```

```cpp
    Node *link;

    public:
        Node(int value)
        {
                info=value;
                link=NULL;
        }
};

typedef Node* NODE;
//C++ function to insert a node at the front end
NODE insert_front(int ele, NODE last)
{
    NODE newnode = new Node(ele);

    if(last==NULL)
        last=newnode;
    else
    newnode→link = last→link;
    last→link=newnode;
    return last;
}


//C++ function to insert a node at the rear end
NODE insert_rear(int ele, NODE last)
{
    NODE newnode = new Node(ele);
    if(last==NULL)
        last=newnode;
    else
    newnode→link = last→link;
    last→link=newnode;
    return newnode;
}


//C++ function to delete a node at the front end
NODE delete_front(NODE last)
{
    NODE temp, first;

    if (last == NULL)
```

```cpp
    {
        cout<<"List is empty"<<endl;
        return NULL;
    }

    if (last→link==last)
    {
        cout<<"element deleted is"<<last→info<<endl;
        delete last;
        return NULL;
    }


    first=last→link;
    last→link=first→link;

    cout<<"element deleted is"<<first→info;
    delete first;

    return last;
}


//C++ function to delete a node at the rear end
NODE delete_rear (NODE last)
{
    NODE prev;

    if (last == NULL)
    {
        cout<<"List is empty"<<endl;
        return NULL;
    }

    if (last→link==last)
    {
        cout<<"element deleted is"<<last→info<<endl;
        delete last;
        return NULL;
    }
    prev=last→link;
    while(prev→link≠ last)
        prev=prev→link;
    prev→link=last→link;
```

```cpp
        cout<<"element deleted is"<<last→info<<endl;
        delete last;

        return prev;
}


//C++ function to display the elements of Circular Singly Linked List
void display(NODE last)
{
        NODE temp;

        if (last == NULL)
        {
                cout<<"List is empty"<<endl;
                return;
        }

        cout<<"Contents of list are"<<endl;
        temp=last→link;

        while (temp≠last)
        {
                cout<<temp→info<<endl;
                temp=temp→link;
        }
        cout<<temp→info<<endl;
}


//Main function

int main()
{
        NODE last;
        last=NULL;
        int ele,key,choice;
        for(;;)
        {
                cout<<"1.Display the contents"<<endl<<
                        "2.Add  at the beginning"<<endl<<
                        "3.Add at the end"<<endl<<
                        "4. Delete_front"<<endl<<
                        "5.Delete_rear"<<endl<<
                        "6.Exit."<<endl;
```

```cpp
            cout<<"Enter your choice: "<<endl;
            cin>>choice;
            switch(choice)
            {
                case 1:
                        display(last);
                        break;
                case 2:
                        cout<<"enter the element to be inserted"<<endl;
                        cin>>ele;
                        last=insert_front(ele,last);
                        break;
                case 3:
                        cout<<"enter the element to be inserted"<<endl;
                        cin>>ele;
                        last=insert_rear(ele,last);
                        break;
                case 4:
                        last=delete_front(last);
                        break;
                case 5:
                        last=delete_rear(last);
                        break;
                case 6: exit(0);
                default: cout<<"invalid choice"<<endl;
            }
        }
}
```

Output:

```
1.Display the contents
2.Add  at the beginning
3.Add at the end
4. Delete_front
5.Delete_rear
6.Exit.
Enter your choice:
2
```

enter the element to be inserted
10
1.Display the contents
2.Add at the beginning
3.Add at the end
4. Delete_front
5.Delete_rear
6.Exit.
Enter your choice:
3
enter the element to be inserted
20
1.Display the contents
2.Add at the beginning
3.Add at the end
4. Delete_front
5.Delete_rear
6.Exit.
Enter your choice:
1
Contents of list are
10
20
1.Display the contents
2.Add at the beginning
3.Add at the end
4. Delete_front
5.Delete_rear
6.Exit.
Enter your choice:
4
element deleted is10
1.Display the contents
2.Add at the beginning
3.Add at the end

```
4. Delete_front
5.Delete_rear
6.Exit.
Enter your choice:
1
Contents of list are
20
1.Display the contents
2.Add  at the beginning
3.Add at the end
4. Delete_front
5.Delete_rear
6.Exit.
Enter your choice:
5
element deleted is20
1.Display the contents
2.Add  at the beginning
3.Add at the end
4. Delete_front
5.Delete_rear
6.Exit.
Enter your choice:
1
List is empty
```

3.10   Circular Singly Linked List with Header node

In circular singly linked list, the link field of the last node contains the address of the head node and link field of the head node contains the address of the first node. The info field of the head node contains the metadata. The metadata may contain the count of number of nodes in the list or any other useful information.

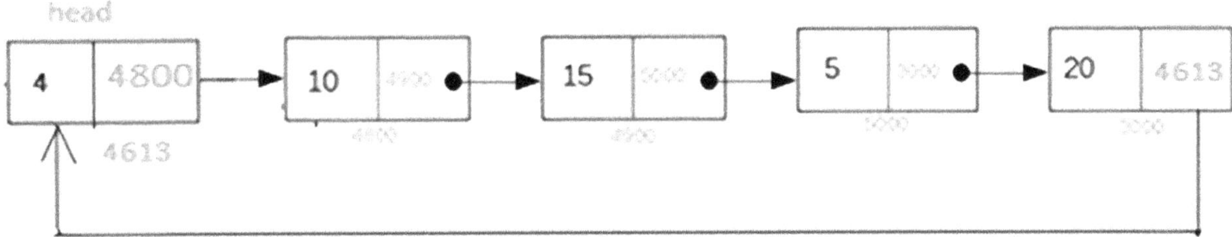

Fig 2.27: *Pictorial representation of Circular Singly Linked List with Header node*

Observe the following points from the above linked list:

- The list contains 4 nodes and each node consists of two fields info and link.
- The first field of each node contains information or data. The info field can contain any type of data like numbers or character or string.
- The second field i.e., link field of each node contains the address of the next node.
- The link field of the last node contains the address of the head node and link field of the head node contains the address of the first node.
- The info field of the head node contains the metadata.

3.11   Operations on Circular Singly Linked Lists

The operations that can be performed on Circular Singly Linked Lists are:

- Inserting a node into the list
- Deleting a node from the list
- Search in a list
- Display the contents of list

3.11.1   Insert a node at the front end

The various steps to be followed to insert a node at the front end:

1. Create a new node named newnode.

```
newnode=new Node(ele);
```

2. Establish a link between newnode and the head node.

```
newnode→link = head→link;
```

3. Make the link field of head node to point to the newnode

```
head→link=newnode;
```

4. Return the address of the head node.

```
return head;
```

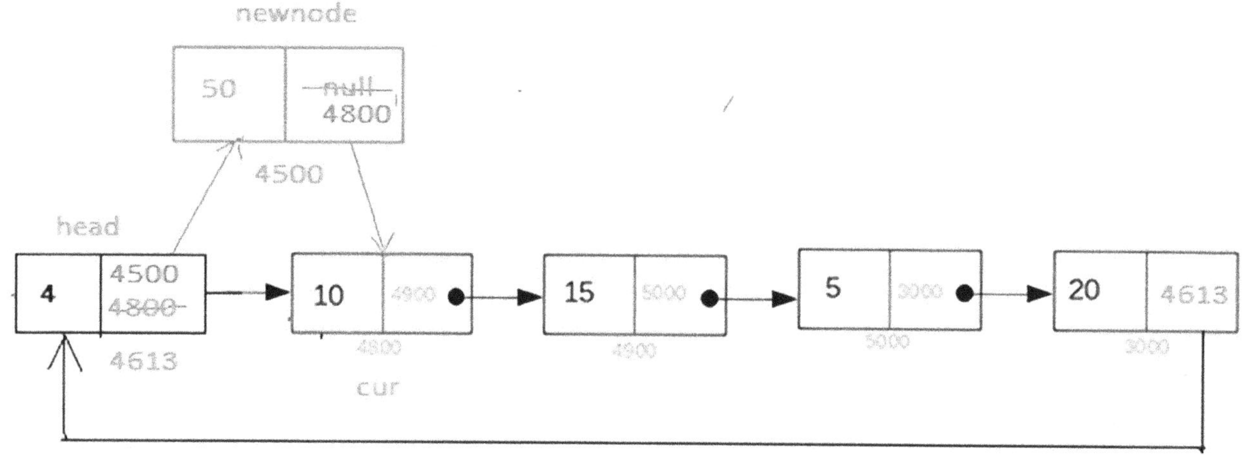

Fig 3.28: *Insert a node at the front end*

```
//C++ function to insert a node at the front end
NODE insert_front(int ele, NODE head)
{
        NODE newnode,cur;

        newnode=new Node(ele);

        cur=head→link;
        newnode→link = cur;
        head→link=newnode;
        return head;
}
```

3.11.2   Insert a node at the rear end

The various steps to be followed to insert a node at the rear end:

1. Create a new node named newnode.

```
        newnode=new Node(ele);
```

2. Find the last node in the link. This can be done by traversing through the list using the pointer say cur until cur->link==head

```
        cur= head→link;
        while(cur→link ≠head)
        {
                cur=cur→link;
        }
```

Create a link between newly created node i.e newnode and cur.

```
cur→link = newnode;
        newnode→link=head;
```

Return the address of the first node

```
        return head;
```

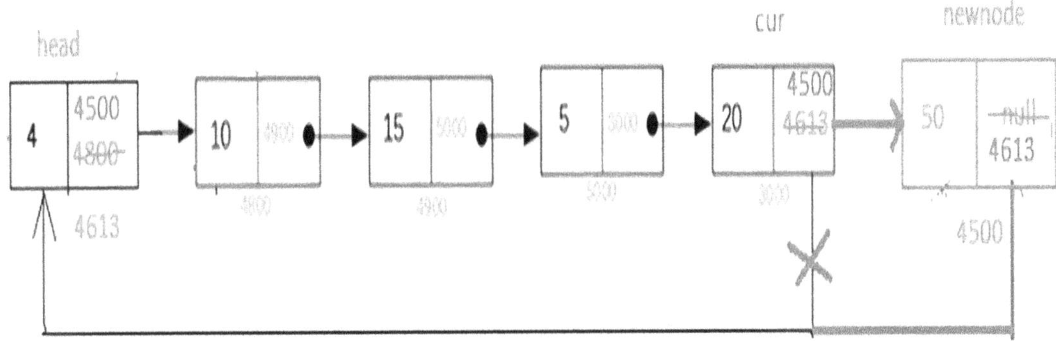

Fig 3.29: *Insert a node at the rear end*

```
//C++ function to insert a node at the rear end
NODE insert_rear(int ele, NODE head)
{
      NODE newnode,cur;

      newnode=new Node(ele);

      cur= head→link;
      while(cur→link ≠head)
      {
            cur=cur→link;
      }
      newnode→link=head;
      cur→link = newnode;
      return head;
}
```

3.11.3 Insert a node after the given key element

The various steps to be followed to insert a node after the given key element:

1. Create a new node named newnode

```
newnode=new Node(ele);
```

2. List is empty.

If list is empty, there are no nodes to compare with the key element, just print the message list is empty.

```
if(head→link==head)
{
        cout<<"List empty, cannot insert element"<<endl;
        return;
}
```

If list is not empty and cur->info == key

```
cur=head;
while (cur→link ≠head)
{
        if(cur→info==key)
        {
                1. newnode-link=cur→link;
                2. cur→link=newnode;
        }
        cur=cur→link;
}
```

Return the head node

```
return head;
```

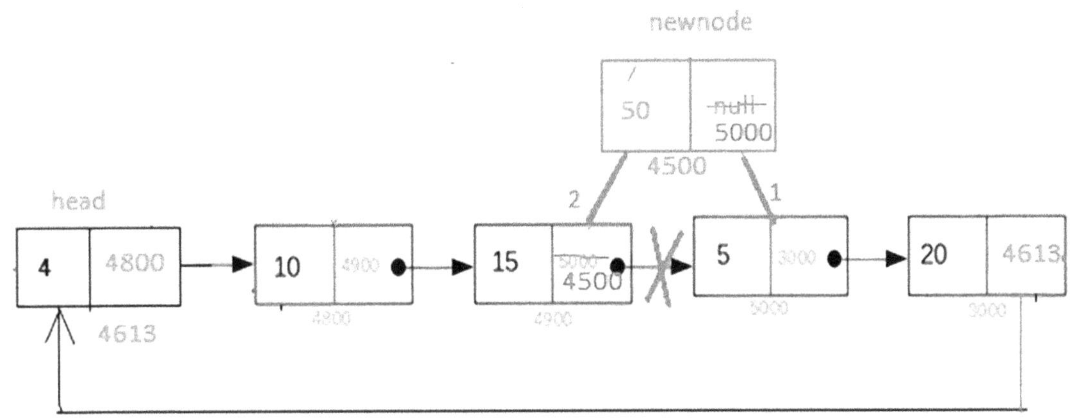

Fig 3.30: Insert a node after the given key element

```cpp
// C++ function Insert a node after the given key element
NODE add_after_key(int ele, int key, NODE head)
{

    NODE newnode, cur;

    newnode=new Node(ele);

    if(head→link==head)
    {
        cout<<"List empty, cannot insert element"<<endl;
        return NULL;
    }
    cur=head→link;
    while(cur→link ≠head)
        {
        if(cur→info==key)
        {
                newnode→link=cur→link;
                cur→link=newnode;
        }
        cur=cur→link;
    }
    return head;
}
```

3.11.4   Insert a node before the given key element

The various steps to be followed to insert a node before the given key element:

1. Create a new node named newnode

```
newnode=new Node(ele);
```

2. List is empty.

If list is empty, there are no nodes to compare with the key element, just print the message list is empty.

```
if(head→link==head)
{
        cout<<"List empty, cannot insert element"<<endl;
        return NULL;
}
```

3. If list is not empty and cur->info==key

We use two pointers cur and prev.

We initialize cur to head node and prev to NULL. We go on traversing through the list until cur. info = key

```
while(cur≠head)
{
     prev=cur;
     if(cur→info==key)
     {
             newnode→link=cur;
             prev→link=newnode;
     }
     cur=cur→link;
}
```

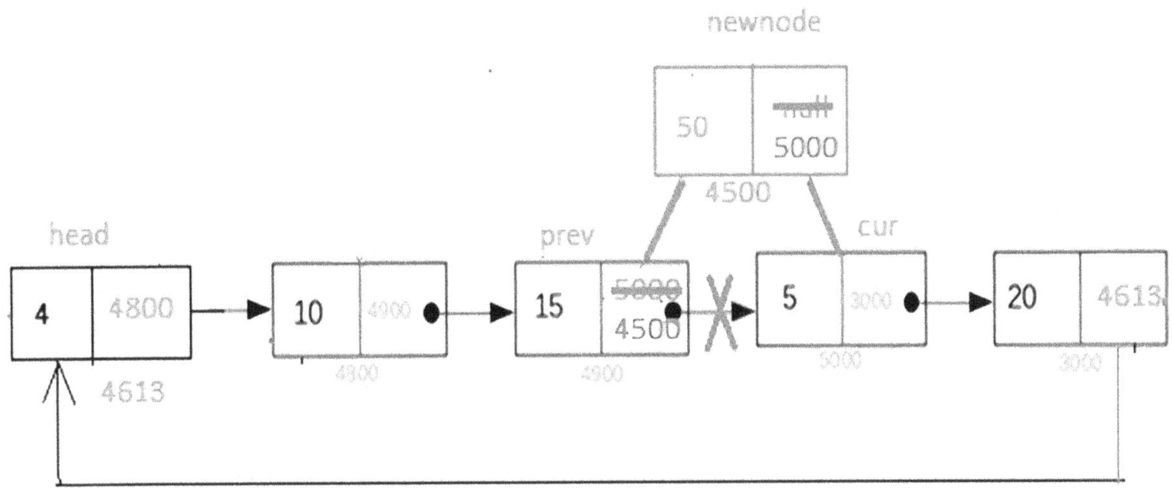

Fig 3.31: *Insert a node before the given key element*

```cpp
// C++ function Insert a node before the given key element
NODE add_bef_key(int ele, int key, NODE head)
{
    NODE newnode, cur,prev;
    newnode=new Node(ele);

    if(head→link==head)
    {
        cout<<"List empty, cannot insert element"<<endl;
        return NULL;
    }
    cur=head→link;
    prev=NULL;

    while(cur→link≠head)
    {
        if(cur→info==key)
        {
            newnode→link=cur;
            prev→link=newnode;
        }
        prev=cur;
    cur=cur→link;
    }
    return head;
}
```

3.11.5   Delete a node from front end

The various steps to be followed to delete a node from front end are:

A temporary variable called temp to be pointed to the link of the head node.

```
temp = head→link;
```

A temporary variable called next to be pointed to the link of the temp node.

```
next=temp→link;
```

Establish a link between the head node and next node

```
head→link=next;
```

Delete the temp node

```
delete temp;
```

Return the head node to the calling function.

```
return head;
```

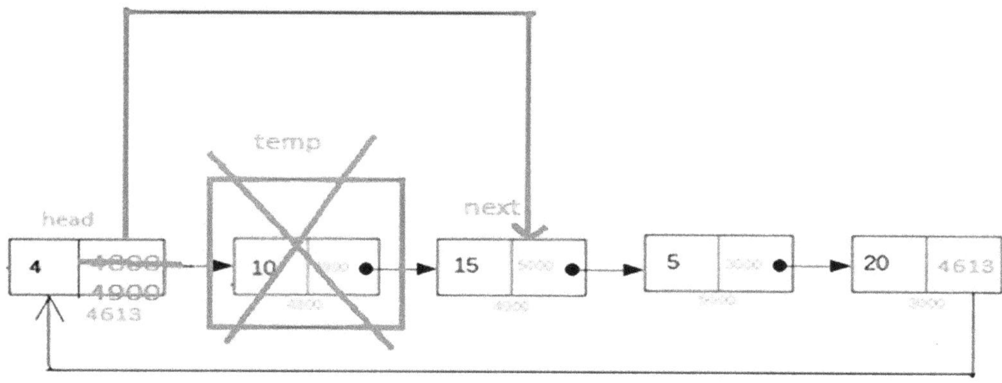

Fig 3.32: Delete a node from front end

```
// C++ function to delete an element from the front end:
NODE delete_front(NODE head)
{
    NODE temp, next;

    if(head→link==head)
    {
```

```cpp
        cout<<"Cannot delete as list is empty"<<endl;
        return head;
    }

    temp = head→link;
    next=temp→link;
    head→link=next;
    cout<<"element deleted is"<<temp→info<<endl;

    delete temp;;
    return head;
}
```

3.11.6   Delete a node from the rear end

The various steps to be followed to delete a node from rear end are:

Consider two variables prev and cur.

```cpp
        prev=NULL;
        cur=head;
```

Traverse through the list until cur points to the last node and prev points to the previous node of cur

```cpp
        while(cur→link≠head)
        {
                prev=cur;
                cur=cur→link;
        }
```

Establish a link between prev node and head node.

```cpp
        prev→link=cur→link;
```

Delete cur node

```cpp
        free(cur);
```

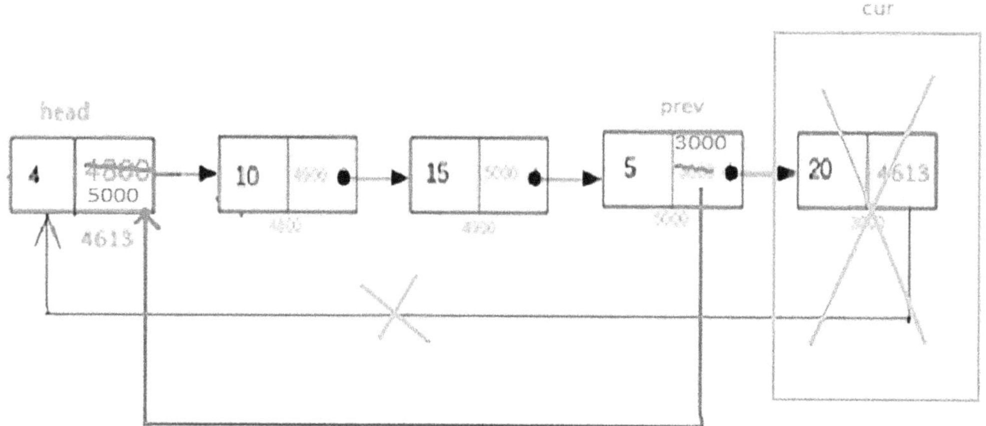

Fig 3.33: *To delete an element from the rear end*

```cpp
// C++ function to delete an element from the rear end:
NODE delete_rear(NODE head)
{

    NODE newnode, cur,prev;
    newnode=new Node(ele);

    if(head→link==head)
    {
        cout<<"List empty, cannot insert element"<<endl;
        return NULL;
    }
    cur=head→link;
    prev=NULL;

    while(cur→link≠head)
    {
        if(cur→info==key)
        {
            newnode→link=cur;
            prev→link=newnode;
        }
        prev=cur;
    cur=cur→link;
    }
    return head;
}
```

3.11.7 Display the elements of the circular singly linked list

```cpp
//C++ function to display the elements of the circular singly linked list
void display(NODE head)
{
    NODE temp;
    if(head→link == head)
    {
        cout<<"LIST is empty"<<endl;
        return;
    }
    cout<<"Contents of the list is"<<endl;
    temp=head→link;
    while(temp≠head)
    {
        cout<<temp→info<<endl;
        temp=temp→link;
    }

}
```

3.11.8 Search for the given key element in the circular singly linked list

```cpp
//C++ function to search for the given key element in the circular singly linked
List
void search(int key,NODE head)
{
    NODE temp;
    if(head→link == head)
    {
        cout<<"LIST is empty"<<endl;
        return;
    }
    temp=head→link;
    while(temp→link≠head)
    {
        if(key==temp→info)
        break;
        temp=temp→link;
    }
```

```cpp
    if(temp→link==head)
    {
            cout<<"element not found"<<endl;
            return;
    }
    cout<<"element found"<<endl;
}
```

3.12   C++ Program to implement the operations of Circular Singly Linked List

```cpp
#include<iostream>
using namespace std;
//Create a class Node
class Node
{
    public:
    int info;
    Node *link;

    public:
        Node(int value)
        {
                info=value;
                link=NULL;
        }
};

typedef Node *NODE;

//C++ function to insert an element at the front end of the list:
NODE insert_front(int ele, NODE head)
{
    NODE newnode,cur;

    newnode=new Node(ele);

    cur=head→link;
    newnode→link = cur;
    head→link=newnode;
```

```cpp
    return head;
}

//C++ function to insert a node at the rear end
NODE insert_rear(int ele, NODE head)
{
    NODE newnode,cur;

    newnode=new Node(ele);

    cur= head→link;
    while(cur→link ≠head)
    {
        cur=cur→link;
    }
    newnode→link=head;
    cur→link = newnode;
    return head;
}

// C++ function Insert a node after the given key element
NODE add_after_key(int ele, int key, NODE head)
{
    NODE newnode, cur;

    newnode=new Node(ele);

    if(head→link==head)
    {
        cout<<"List empty, cannot insert element"<<endl;
        return NULL;
    }
    cur=head→link;
    while(cur→link ≠head)
    {
        if(cur→info==key)
        {
            newnode→link=cur→link;
            cur→link=newnode;
        }
        cur=cur→link;
    }
```

```cpp
        return head;
}


// C++ function Insert a node before the given key element

NODE add_bef_key(int ele, int key, NODE head)
{

        NODE newnode, cur,prev;
        newnode=new Node(ele);

        if(head→link==head)
        {
                cout<<"List empty, cannot insert element"<<endl;
                return NULL;
        }
        cur=head→link;
        prev=NULL;

        while(cur→link≠head)
    {
                if(cur→info==key)
                {
                        newnode→link=cur;
                        prev→link=newnode;
                }
                prev=cur;
        cur=cur→link;
    }
        return head;
}
// C++ function to delete an element from the front end:
NODE delete_front(NODE head)
{
        NODE temp, next;

        if(head→link==head)
        {
                cout<<"Cannot delete as list is empty"<<endl;
                return head;
        }
```

```cpp
    temp = head→link;
    next=temp→link;
    head→link=next;
    cout<<"element deleted is"<<temp→info<<endl;

    delete temp;;
    return head;
}
// C++ function to delete an element from the rear end:
NODE delete_rear(NODE head)
{
    NODE cur,prev,temp;
    if(head→link==head)
    {
        cout<<"Cannot delete as list is empty"<<endl;
        return head;
    }
    prev=NULL;
    cur=head→link;
    while(cur→link≠head)
    {
        prev=cur;
        cur=cur→link;
    }
    prev→link=head;
    cout<<"element deleted is"<<cur→info<<endl;

    delete cur;
    return head;
}
//C++ function to display the elements of the circular singly linked list
void display(NODE head)
{
    NODE temp;
    if(head→link == head)
    {
        cout<<"LIST is empty"<<endl;
        return;
    }
    cout<<"Contents of the list is"<<endl;
    temp=head→link;
    while(temp≠head)
```

```cpp
        {
                cout<<temp→info<<endl;
                temp=temp→link;
        }

}
//C++ function to search for the given key element in the circular singly linked
list
void search(int key,NODE head)
{
        NODE temp;
        if(head→link == head)
        {
                cout<<"LIST is empty"<<endl;
                return;
        }
        temp=head→link;
        while(temp→link≠head)
        {
                if(key==temp→info)
                break;
                temp=temp→link;
        }
        if(temp→link==head)
        {
                cout<<"element not found"<<endl;
                return;
        }
        cout<<"element found"<<endl;
}

// Main function
int main()
{
        NODE head;
        head = new Node(0);
        head→link=head;

        int ele,key,choice;
        for(;;)
        {
```

```cpp
cout<<"1.Display the contents"<<endl<<
    "2.Add  at the beginning"<<endl<<
    "3.Add at the end"<<endl<<
    "4. Delete_front"<<endl<<
    "5.Delete_rear"<<endl<<
    "6.Search"<<endl<<
    "7.Add after key"<<endl<<
    "8. Add before key"<<endl<<
  "9.Exit."<<endl;
cout<<"Enter your choice: "<<endl;
cin>>choice;
switch(choice)
{
    case 1:
        display(head);
        break;
    case 2:
        cout<<"enter the element to be inserted"<<endl;
        cin>>ele;
        head=insert_front(ele,head);
        break;
    case 3:
        cout<<"enter the element to be inserted"<<endl;
        cin>>ele;
        head=insert_rear(ele,head);
        break;
    case 4:
        head=delete_front(head);
        break;
    case 5:
        head=delete_rear(head);
        break;
    case 6:
        cout<<"enter the element to be searched"<<endl;
        cin>>key;
        search(key,head);
        break;
    case 7:
        cout<<"enter the element to be inserted"<<endl;
        cin>>ele;
        cout<<"enter the key element"<<endl;
        cin>>key;
```

```cpp
                        head=add_after_key(ele,key,head);
                        break;
                case 8:
                        cout<<"enter the element to be inserted"<<endl;
                        cin>>ele;
                        cout<<"enter the key element"<<endl;
                        cin>>key;
                        head=add_bef_key(ele,key,head);
                        break;
                default:
                        cout<<"invalid choice"<<endl;

                }
        }
}
```

```
Output:
1.Display the contents
2.Add   at the beginning
3.Add at the end
4. Delete_front
5.Delete_rear
6.Search
7.Add after key
8. Add before key
9.Exit.
Enter your choice:
2
enter the element to be inserted
10
1.Display the contents
2.Add   at the beginning
3.Add at the end
4. Delete_front
5.Delete_rear
6.Search
7.Add after key
8. Add before key
9.Exit.
Enter your choice:
3
enter the element to be inserted
```

```
20
1.Display the contents
2.Add  at the beginning
3.Add at the end
4. Delete_front
5.Delete_rear
6.Search
7.Add after key
8. Add before key
9.Exit.
Enter your choice:
1
Contents of the list is
10
20
1.Display the contents
2.Add  at the beginning
3.Add at the end
4. Delete_front
5.Delete_rear
6.Search
7.Add after key
8. Add before key
9.Exit.
Enter your choice:
7
enter the element to be inserted
15
enter the key element
10
1.Display the contents
2.Add  at the beginning
3.Add at the end
4. Delete_front
5.Delete_rear
6.Search
7.Add after key
8. Add before key
9.Exit.
Enter your choice:
8
enter the element to be inserted
```

```
18
enter the key element
15
1.Display the contents
2.Add  at the beginning
3.Add at the end
4. Delete_front
5.Delete_rear
6.Search
7.Add after key
8. Add before key
9.Exit.
Enter your choice:
1
Contents of the list is
10
18
15
20
1.Display the contents
2.Add  at the beginning
3.Add at the end
4. Delete_front
5.Delete_rear
6.Search
7.Add after key
8. Add before key
9.Exit.
Enter your choice:
6
enter the element to be searched
15
element found
1.Display the contents
2.Add  at the beginning
3.Add at the end
4. Delete_front
5.Delete_rear
6.Search
7.Add after key
8. Add before key
9.Exit.
```

```
Enter your choice:
4
element deleted is10
1.Display the contents
2.Add  at the beginning
3.Add at the end
4. Delete_front
5.Delete_rear
6.Search
7.Add after key
8. Add before key
9.Exit.
Enter your choice:
5
element deleted is20
```

3.13 List of questions

1. Construct a C++ Program to perform the below functions on singly linked list without header node:

   - createList( )
   - isEmpty( )
   - size( )
   - addFirst( )
   - addLast( )
   - addAtPosition( )
   - addAfterKey( )
   - addBeforeKey( )
   - removeFirst( )
   - removeLast( )
   - removeAtPosition( )
   - removeAfterKey( )
   - removeBeforeKey( )
   - display( )
   - search( )

2. Construct a C++ Program to perform the below functions on circular singly linked list without header node:

- createList( )
- isEmpty( )
- size( )
- addFirst( )
- addLast( )
- addAtPosition( )
- addAfterKey( )
- addBeforeKey( )
- removeFirst( )
- removeLast( )
- removeAtPosition( )
- removeAfterKey( )
- removeBeforeKey( )
- display( )
- search( )

3. Construct a C++ Program to perform the below functions on circular singly linked List with header node:

- createList( )
- isEmpty( )
- size( )
- addFirst( )
- addLast( )
- addAtPosition( )
- addAfterKey( )
- addBeforeKey( )
- removeFirst( )
- removeLast( )
- removeAtPosition( )
- removeAfterKey( )
- removeBeforeKey( )
- display( )
- search( )

4. Construct a C++ Program to perform the below functions on singly linked List with header node:

- createList( )
- isEmpty( )
- size( )
- addFirst( )
- addLast( )
- addAtPosition( )
- addAfterKey( )
- addBeforeKey( )
- removeFirst( )
- removeLast( )
- removeAtPosition( )
- removeAfterKey( )
- removeBeforeKey( )
- display( )
- search( )

CHAPTER - 4

Chapter 4

Doubly Linked List

Introduction

Singly Linked List finds its applications in implementing stacks and queues but has its own disadvantages. The disadvantages of singly linked list can be overcome by the doubly linked list. Linked list finds its applications in real time like image viewer, web pages, music player and many more. Hence it is very much necessary to know this doubly linked list data structure.

Structure

- Advantages of Singly Linked List
- Disadvantages of Singly Linked List
- Doubly Linked List with header with operations
- Circular Doubly Linked List with header with operations

Objectives:

After reading this chapter, the reader can implement the various operations of doubly linked list and circular singly list. In this chapter, implementation of various operations of doubly linked list and circular singly list is discussed in detail with proper diagrams. The programs given here are thoroughly tested and debugged. This chapter will help the reader in writing efficient programs using Linked list data structure.

4.1 Advantages and Disadvantages of Singly Linked List

The advantages and disadvantages of Singly Linked List are discussed in the below sections

4.1.1 Advantages of Singly Linked List

The various advantages of Singly Linked List are as discussed below:

- **Insertion and Deletion at the Beginning is efficient**–Inserting or deleting an element at the beginning of the list is fast. This is because only a pointer first or head needs to be updated.

- **Implementation is simple** – Singly linked lists are simple to implement and understand. With just one pointer pointing to the next element in the list, the insertion and deletion of nodes can be done in a simple way.
- **Space Efficiency** – Singly linked lists make use of single reference for the next node i.e., there can be single data field and link field. Hence the space consumed is less when compared to other data structures.
- **Traversal through the list is easy** – Singly linked lists offer flexible traversal options since the traversal is done from start or first node till the end of list is reached.
- **Dynamic Allocation:** Singly linked lists make use of dynamic allocation function to allocate and deallocate memory. As a result of which the memory can be reduced or expanded during run time.

4.1.2   Disadvantages of Singly Linked List

The various disadvantages of Singly Linked List are as discussed below:

- **Accessing elements:** Since the singly linked list make use of single pointer to the next node, accessing the previous nodes is not possible and it is necessary to traverse through the list.
- **Extra Memory Overhead** – Singly linked lists require an additional pointer to know the details of previous nodes where extra memory has to be allocated for the pointers. This has been overcome in other data structures.
- **Deletion Operations is quite tedious job** – Deleting an element in a singly linked list is tedious when compared to other data structures.

4.2   Doubly linked list with header node

A doubly linked list is a linear collection of nodes where each node is divided into three nodes:

- info / data -This field contains data or information to be stored.
- llink / prev – This field contains the address of the previous node or the left node
- rlink / next – This field contains the address of the next node or the right node.
- rlink and llink are the pointer fields since both the field stores the address of the next and previous node respectively.

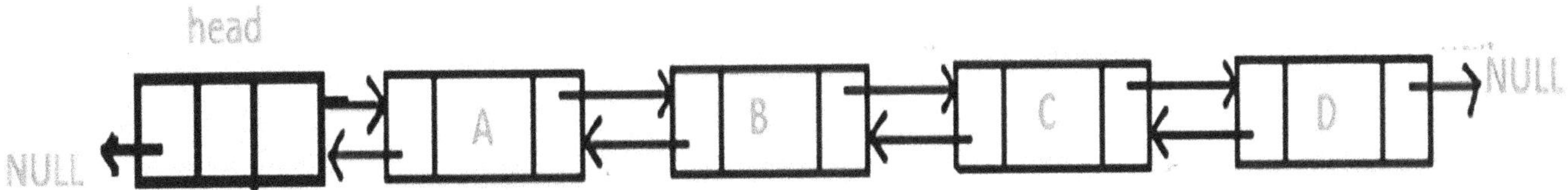

Fig 4.1: Pictorial representation of Doubly Linked List

Observe the following points from the above linked list:

- The list contains 4 nodes and each node consists of three fields info llink and rlink.
- The first field i.e., llink field of each node contains the address of the previous node.
- The second field of each node contains information or data. The info field can contain any type of data like numbers or character or string.
- The third field i.e., rlink field of each node contains the address of the next node.
- The rlink field of last node and llink field of first node contains NULL.

4.3　Operations on Doubly Linked Lists

The operations that can be performed on Doubly Linked Lists are:

- Inserting a node into the list
- Deleting a node from the list
- Search in a list
- Display the contents of list

4.3.1　Insert a node at the front end

The various steps to be followed to insert a node at the front end:

Step 1: Create a new node named newnode

```
newnode=new Node(ele);
```

Step 2: The node newnode can be inserted at the front end using the following step:

```
cur=head;
cur=head→rlink;
head→rlink=newnode;
newnode→llink=head;
newnode→rlink=cur;
cur→llink=newnode;
```

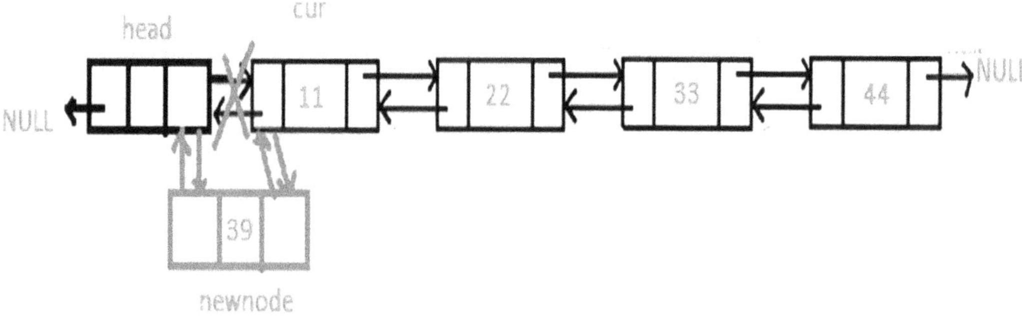

Fig 4.2: *Insert a node at the front end of Doubly Linked List*

```
// C++ function to insert a node at the front end of Doubly Linked List
NODE insert_front(int ele, NODE head)
{
        NODE newnode, cur;

        newnode=new Node(ele);

        if(head→rlink==NULL)
        {
            newnode→llink=head;
            head→rlink=newnode;
            return head;
        }

        cur=head→rlink;
        head→rlink=newnode;
        newnode→llink=head;

        newnode→rlink=cur;
        cur→llink=newnode;

        return head;
}
```

4.3.2   Insert a node at the rear end

The various steps to be followed to insert a node at the rear end:

Step 1: Create a new node named newnode

```
newnode=new Node(ele);
```

Step 2: The node newnode can be inserted at the front end using the following step:

```
cur=head;
while(cu→rlink≠null)
{
        cur=cur→rlink;
}
cur→rlink=newnode;
newnode→llink=cur;
```

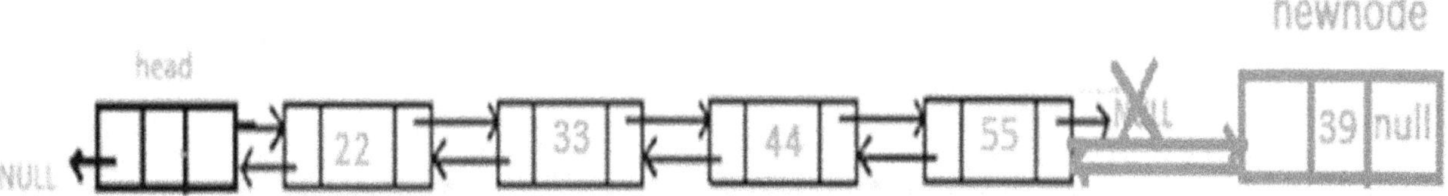

Fig 4.3: *Insert a node at the rear end of Doubly Linked List*

```cpp
// C++ function to insert a node at the rear end of Doubly Linked List
NODE insert_rear(int ele, NODE head)
{
    NODE newnode, cur;
    newnode=new Node(ele);
    if(head→rlink==NULL)
    {
        newnode→llink=head;
        head→rlink=newnode;
        return head;
    }
    cur=head→rlink;
    while(cur→rlink≠NULL)
    {
        cur=cur→rlink;
    }
    cur→rlink=newnode;
    newnode→llink=cur;
    return head;
}
```

4.3.3   Delete a node from front end

The various steps to be followed to delete a node from front end are:

Step 1: A temporary variable called temp and cur to be pointed as shown below:

```cpp
temp = head→rlink;
cur=temp→rlink;
```

Step 2: establish a connection between the head node and the temp->rlink node.

```cpp
head→rlink=cur;
cur→llink=head;
```

Step 3: delete the temp node

```
delete temp;
```

Step 4: return the head node to the calling function.

```
return head;
```

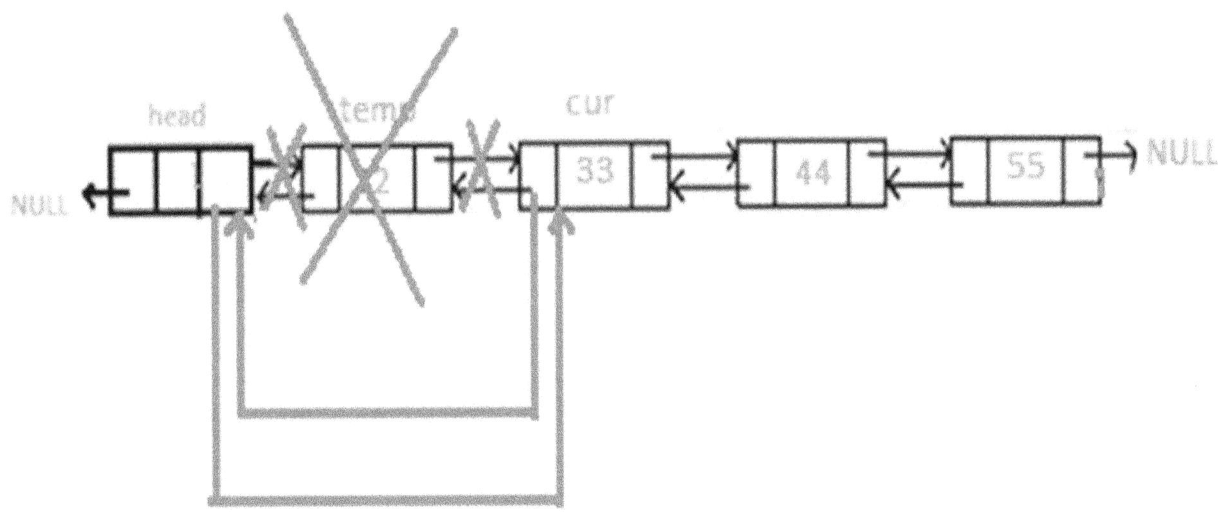

Fig 4.4: Delete a node at the front end of Doubly Linked List

```cpp
// C++ function to delete a node at the front end of Doubly Linked List
NODE delete_front(NODE head)
{
    NODE cur,temp;
    if(head==NULL)
    {
        cout<<"List empty"<<endl;
        return NULL;
    }
    temp = head→rlink;
    cur=temp→rlink;
cout<<"element deleted is "<<temp→info<<endl;
head→rlink=cur;
    cur→llink=head;
    delete temp;
    return head;
}
```

4.3.4   Delete a node from rear end

The various steps to be followed to delete a node from rear end are:

Step 1: initialize two pointers cur and prev as shown below:

```
cur=head;
prev=NULL;
```
Step 2: Traverse through the list until cur→rlink points to NULL;
```
while(cur→rlink ≠NULL)
{
        prev=cur;
        cur=cur→rlink;
}
```
Step 3: delete the last node cur from the list
```
printf("element deleted = %d\n, cur→info);
prev→rlink=NULL;
free(cur);
```
Step 4: Return the head node
```
return head;
```

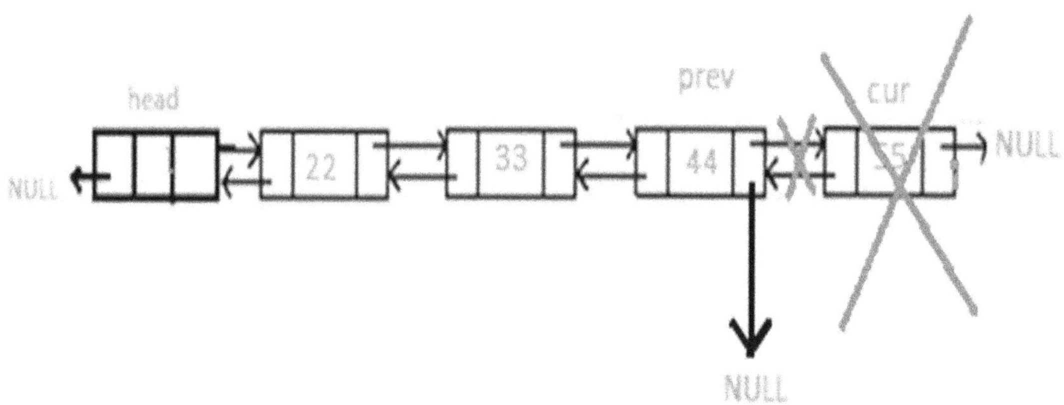

Fig 4.5: *Delete a node at the rear end of Doubly Linked List*

```
// C++ function to delete a node at the rear end of Doubly Linked List
NODE delete_rear(NODE head)
{
    NODE cur,prev;
    if(head→rlink==NULL)
    {
        cout<<"List empty"<<endl;
        return NULL;
    }
```

```cpp
    cur=head;
    prev=NULL;
    while(cur→rlink ≠NULL)
    {
        prev=cur;
        cur=cur→rlink;
  }
        cout<<"element deleted is "<<cur→info<<endl;
prev→rlink=NULL;
delete cur;
        return head;
}
```

4.3.5   Display the elements of the Doubly Linked List

```cpp
//C++ function to display the elements of the Doubly Linked List
void display(NODE head)
{
    NODE temp;

    if(head→rlink==NULL)
    {
        cout<<"List empty"<<endl;
        return;
    }

    cout<<"Contents of the list is "<<endl;
    temp=head→rlink;

  while(temp≠NULL)
    {
        cout<<temp→info<<endl;
        temp=temp→rlink;
    }


}
```

4.3.6   Search for the elements in the Doubly Linked List

```
//C++ function to search for the given key element in the doubly linked list
void search(int key,NODE head)
{
    NODE temp;
    if(head→rlink == NULL)
    {
        cout<<"List empty"<<endl;
        return;
    }
    temp=head→rlink;
  while(temp≠NULL)
    {
        if(key==temp→info)
        break;
        temp=temp→rlink;
    }
    if(temp==NULL)
    {
        cout<<"element not found"<<endl;
        return;
    }
    cout<<"element found"<<endl;
}
```

4.3.7   Insert a node before the given key element:

The various steps to be followed to insert a node before the given key element:

Step 1: Create a new node named newnode

```
        NODE newnode;
        newnode=new Node(ele);
```

Step 2: List is empty.

If list is empty, there are no nodes to compare with the key element, just print the message list is empty.

```
        if(head→rlink==NULL)
        {
```

```
        cout<<"List empty, cannot insert element"<<endl;
        return NULL;
    }
```

Step 3: Initialsie cur with head and traverse through the end of the list and if in case key is found follow the below steps:

```
cur=head;
while(cur→rlink≠null)
{
if(cur→info==key)
{
        newnode→llinkcur→link;
        newnode→rlink=cur→llink;
        cur→llink=newnode→rlink;
        head→rlink=newnode→llink;
}
cur=cur→rlink;
}
```

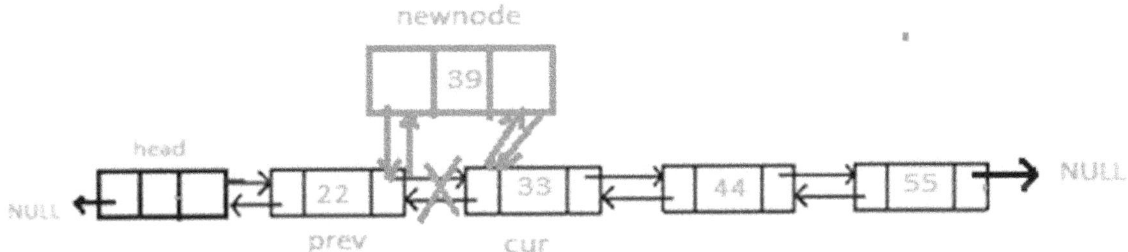

Fig 4.6: Insert a node before the given key element

```cpp
// C++ function to insert a node before the given key element
NODE add_bef_key(int ele, int key, NODE head)
{
    NODE newnode, cur,prev;
    newnode=new Node(ele);
    if(head→rlink==NULL)
    {
        cout<<"List empty, cannot insert element"<<endl;
    return NULL;
```

```
}
cur=head→rlink;
prev=NULL;
while(cur≠NULL)
{
        if(cur→info==key)
        {
                newnode→rlink=cur;
                newnode→llink=prev;
                cur→llink=newnode;
                prev→rlink=newnode;
                return head;
        }
        prev=cur;
        cur=cur→rlink;
}
if(cur== NULL)
{
        cout<<"key not found"<<endl;
        return head;
}
return head;
}
```

4.3.8   Insert a node after the given key element:

The various steps to be followed to insert a node after the given key element:

Step 1: Create a new node named newnode

```
newnode=new Node(ele);
```

Step 2: List is empty.

If list is empty, there are no nodes to compare with the key element, just print the message list is empty.

```
if(head→rlink==NULL)
{
        cout<<"List empty, cannot insert element"<<endl;
        return NULL;
}
```

Step 3: If list is not empty and cur.info == key

```
cur=NULL;
next=head
while (cur→rlink ≠NULL)
{
        if(cur→info==key)
        {
                newnode→llink=cur;
                cur→rlink=newnode;
                newnode→rlink=next;
                next→llink=newnode;
        }
        cur=next;
        next=next→rlink;
}
```

Step 4: return the head node

```
return head;
```

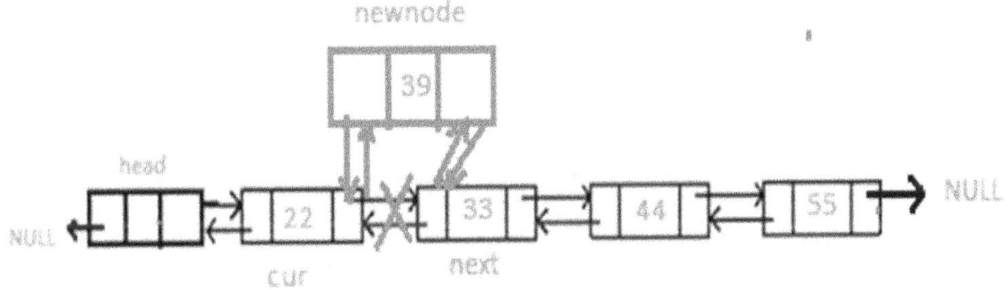

Fig 4.7: *Insert a node after the given key element*

```cpp
// C++ function to insert a node after the given key element
NODE add_after_key(int ele, int key, NODE head)
{
    NODE newnode, cur, next;
    newnode= new Node(ele);
    if(head→rlink==NULL)
{
    cout<<"List empty, cannot insert element"<<endl;
return NULL;
```

```
}
cur=head→rlink;
next=NULL;
while (cur≠NULL)
{
            if(cur→info==key)
            {
                    cur→rlink→llink=newnode;
                    newnode→rlink=cur→rlink;
                    cur→rlink=newnode;
                    newnode→llink=cur;
                    return head;
        }
            cur=cur→rlink;
}
if(cur== NULL)
    {
        cout<<"key not found"<<endl;
        return head;
    }
    return head;
}
```

4.4   C++ Program to implement the operations of Doubly Linked List with header node

```
#include<iostream>
using namespace std;

class Node
{
    public:
    int info;
    Node *llink;
    Node *rlink;

    public:
        Node(int value)
            {
```

```cpp
                    info=value;
                    llink=NULL;
                    rlink=NULL;
                }
};

typedef Node* NODE;

// C++ function to insert a node at the front end of Doubly Linked List
NODE insert_front(int ele, NODE head)
{
        NODE newnode, cur;

        newnode=new Node(ele);

        if(head→rlink==NULL)
        {
            newnode→llink=head;
            head→rlink=newnode;
            return head;
        }

        cur=head→rlink;
        head→rlink=newnode;
        newnode→llink=head;

        newnode→rlink=cur;
        cur→llink=newnode;

        return head;
}

// C++ function to insert a node at the rear end of Doubly Linked List
NODE insert_rear(int ele, NODE head)
{
        NODE newnode, cur;

        newnode=new Node(ele);

        if(head→rlink==NULL)
        {
```

```cpp
        newnode→llink=head;
        head→rlink=newnode;
        return head;
    }

    cur=head→rlink;

while(cur→rlink≠NULL)
{
        cur=cur→rlink;
}
cur→rlink=newnode;
newnode→llink=cur;

    return head;
}


// C++ function to delete a node at the front end of Doubly Linked List
NODE delete_front(NODE head)
{
    NODE cur,temp;
    if(head==NULL)
    {
        cout<<"List empty"<<endl;
        return NULL;
    }
temp = head→rlink;
cur=temp→rlink;
  cout<<"element deleted is "<<temp→info<<endl;

    head→rlink=cur;
    cur→llink=head;

    delete temp;

    return head;
}


// C++ function to delete a node at the rear end of Doubly Linked List
NODE delete_rear(NODE head)
{
    NODE cur,prev;
```

```cpp
    if(head→rlink==NULL)
    {
        cout<<"List empty"<<endl;
        return NULL;
    }

    cur=head;
    prev=NULL;

    while(cur→rlink ≠NULL)
     {
        prev=cur;
        cur=cur→rlink;
     }
        cout<<"element deleted is "<<cur→info<<endl;
     prev→rlink=NULL;

    delete cur;

    return head;
}

//C++ function to display the elements of the Doubly Linked List
void display(NODE head)
{
    NODE temp;

    if(head→rlink==NULL)
    {
        cout<<"List empty"<<endl;
        return;
    }

    cout<<"Contents of the list is "<<endl;
    temp=head→rlink;

    while(temp≠NULL)
     {
        cout<<temp→info<<endl;
        temp=temp→rlink;
     }

}
```

```cpp
//C++ function to search for the given key element in the doubly linked list
void search(int key,NODE head)
{
	NODE temp;

	if(head→rlink == NULL)
	{
		cout<<"List empty"<<endl;
		return;
	}

	temp=head→rlink;

	while(temp≠NULL)
	{
		if(key==temp→info)
		break;
		temp=temp→rlink;
	}

	if(temp==NULL)
	{
		cout<<"element not found"<<endl;
		return;
	}

	cout<<"element found"<<endl;
}

// C++ function to insert a node before the given key element
NODE add_bef_key(int ele, int key, NODE head)
{

	NODE newnode, cur,prev;

	newnode=new Node(ele);

	if(head→rlink==NULL)
	{
		cout<<"List empty, cannot insert element"<<endl;
		return NULL;
```

```cpp
    }
    cur=head→rlink;
    prev=NULL;

    while(cur≠NULL)
    {
        if(cur→info==key)
        {
            newnode→rlink=cur;
            newnode→llink=prev;
            cur→llink=newnode;
            prev→rlink=newnode;
            return head;
        }
        prev=cur;
        cur=cur→rlink;
    }
    if(cur== NULL)
    {
        cout<<"key not found"<<endl;
        return head;
    }
    return head;
}

// C++ function to insert a node after the given key element
NODE add_after_key(int ele, int key, NODE head)
{

    NODE newnode, cur, next;

    newnode= new Node(ele);

    if(head→rlink==NULL)
    {
        cout<<"List empty, cannot insert element"<<endl;
        return NULL;
    }

    cur=head→rlink;
    next=NULL;
```

```cpp
    while (cur≠NULL)
    {
        if(cur→info==key)
        {
            cur→rlink→llink=newnode;
            newnode→rlink=cur→rlink;
            cur→rlink=newnode;
            newnode→llink=cur;
            return head;
        }
        cur=cur→rlink;
    }
    if(cur== NULL)
    {
        cout<<"key not found"<<endl;
        return head;
    }
    return head;
}
//main function
int main()
{
    NODE head;
    int ele,choice,key;
    head=new Node(0);

    for(;;)
    {
        cout<<"1.Display the contents"<<endl<<
              "2.Add   at the beginning"<<endl<<
              "3.Add at the end"<<endl<<
              "4. Delete_front"<<endl<<
              "5.Delete_rear"<<endl<<
              "6.Search"<<endl<<
              "7.Add after key"<<endl<<
              "8. Add before key"<<endl<<
           "9.Exit"<<endl;
        cout<<"Enter your choice: "<<endl;
        cin>>choice;
        switch(choice)
```

```cpp
{
    case 1:
        display(head);
        break;
    case 2:
        cout<<"enter the element to be inserted"<<endl;
        cin>>ele;
        head=insert_front(ele,head);
        break;
    case 3:
        cout<<"enter the element to be inserted"<<endl;
        cin>>ele;
        head=insert_rear(ele,head);
        break;
    case 4:
        head=delete_front(head);
        break;
    case 5:
        head=delete_rear(head);
        break;
    case 6:
        cout<<"enter the element to be searched"<<endl;
        cin>>key;
        search(key,head);
        break;
    case 7:
        cout<<"enter the element to be inserted"<<endl;
        cin>>ele;
        cout<<"enter the key element"<<endl;
        cin>>key;
        head=add_after_key(ele,key,head);
        break;
    case 8:
        cout<<"enter the element to be inserted"<<endl;
        cin>>ele;
        cout<<"enter the key element"<<endl;
        cin>>key;
        head=add_bef_key(ele,key,head);
        break;
    case 9:exit(0);
    default:
```

```cpp
                    cout<<"invalid choice"<<endl;
           }
      }
}
```

Output:
1.Display the contents
2.Add at the beginning
3.Add at the end
4. Delete_front
5.Delete_rear
6.Search
7.Add after key
8. Add before key
9.Exit
Enter your choice:
2
enter the element to be inserted
20
1.Display the contents
2.Add at the beginning
3.Add at the end
4. Delete_front
5.Delete_rear
6.Search
7.Add after key
8. Add before key
9.Exit
Enter your choice:
3
enter the element to be inserted
40
1.Display the contents
2.Add at the beginning
3.Add at the end
4. Delete_front
5.Delete_rear
6.Search
7.Add after key
8. Add before key
9.Exit
Enter your choice:

```
7
enter the element to be inserted
30
enter the key element
20
1.Display the contents
2.Add  at the beginning
3.Add at the end
4. Delete_front
5.Delete_rear
6.Search
7.Add after key
8. Add before key
9.Exit
Enter your choice:
8
enter the element to be inserted
30
enter the key element
40
1.Display the contents
2.Add  at the beginning
3.Add at the end
4. Delete_front
5.Delete_rear
6.Search
7.Add after key
8. Add before key
9.Exit
Enter your choice:
1
Contents of the list is
20
30
30
40
1.Display the contents
2.Add  at the beginning
3.Add at the end
4. Delete_front
5.Delete_rear
6.Search
```

```
7.Add after key
8. Add before key
9.Exit
Enter your choice:
4
element deleted is 20
1.Display the contents
2.Add  at the beginning
3.Add at the end
4. Delete_front
5.Delete_rear
6.Search
7.Add after key
8. Add before key
9.Exit
Enter your choice:
5
element deleted is 40
1.Display the contents
2.Add  at the beginning
3.Add at the end
4. Delete_front
5.Delete_rear
6.Search
7.Add after key
8. Add before key
9.Exit
Enter your choice:
6
enter the element to be searched
30
element found
```

4.5   Circular Doubly Linked List with header node

A circular doubly linked list is a variation of doubly linked list where:

- info / data -This field contains data or information to be stored.
- llink / prev– This field contains the address of the previous node or the left node
- rlink / next – This field contains the address of the next node or the right node.
- The rlink of the last node contains the address of the head node and llink of the head node contains address of the last node.

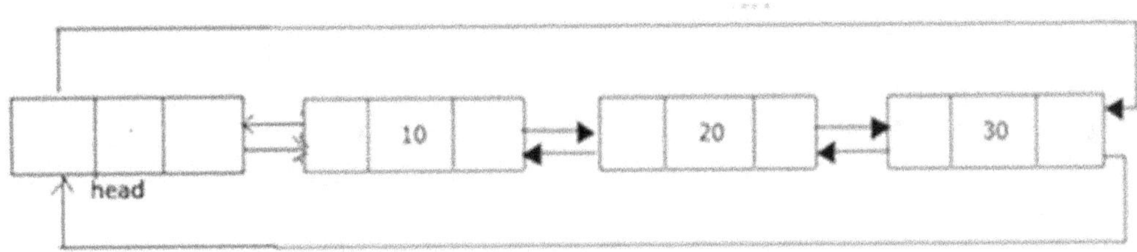

Fig 4.8: *Pictorial representation of Circular Doubly Linked List*

Observe the following points from the above linked list:

- The list contains 4 nodes and each node consists of three fields info, llink and rlink.
- The first field i.e., llink field of each node contains the address of the previous node.
- The second field of each node contains information or data. The info field can contain any type of data like numbers or character or string.
- The third field i.e., rlink field of each node contains the address of the next node.
- The rlink of the last node contains the address of the head node and llink of the head node contains address of the last node.

4.6   Operations on Doubly Linked Lists

The operations that can be performed on Doubly Linked Lists are:

- Inserting a node into the list
- Deleting a node from the list
- Search in a list
- Display the contents of list

4.6.1   Insert a node at the front end

The various steps to be followed to insert a node at the front end:

Step 1: Create a new node named newnode

```
newnode=new Node(ele);
```

Step 2: The node newnode can be inserted at the front end using the following step:

```
cur=head→rlink;
head→rlink = newnode;
newnode→llink=head;
head→rlink=cur;
cur→llink=newnode;
```

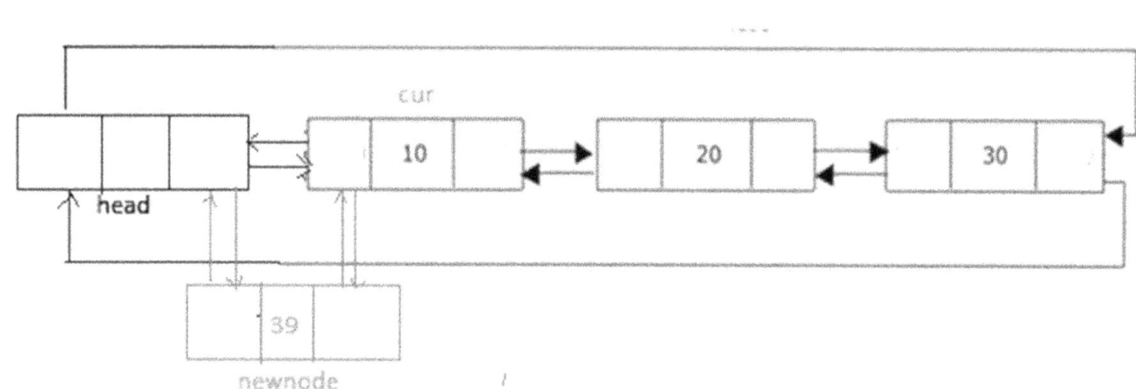

Fig 4.9: *Insert a node at the front end of Doubly Linked List*

```
// C++ function to insert a node at the front end of circular Doubly Linked List
NODE insert_front(int ele, NODE head)
{
        NODE newnode, cur;

        newnode=new Node(ele);

        cur=head→rlink;

        head→rlink=newnode;
        newnode→llink=head;
        newnode→rlink=cur;
        cur→llink=newnode;

        return head;
}
```

4.6.2   Insert a node at the rear end

Insertion of node at the rear end can be explained by the fig below:

Fig 4.10: Insert a node at the rear end of Doubly Linked List

// C++ function to insert a node at the rear end of Doubly Linked List

NODE insert_rear(int ele, NODE head)

{

NODE newnode, cur;

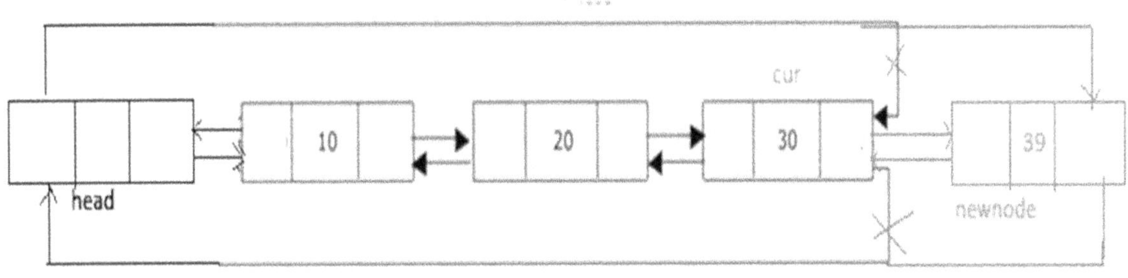

```
        newnode=new Node(ele);
cur=head→llink;
        head→llink=newnode;
        newnode→rlink=head;
        newnode→llink=cur;
        cur→rlink=newnode;
return head;
}
```

4.6.3 Delete a node from the front end

The delete from front end operation can be explained by the below figure:

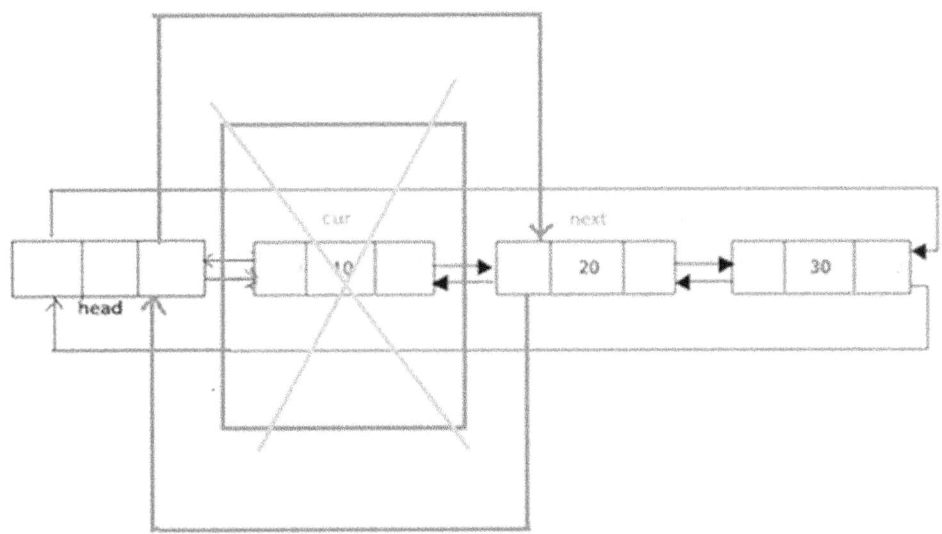

Fig 4.11: Delete a node from the front end

```cpp
// C++ function to  Delete a node from the front end:
NODE delete_front(NODE head)
{
    NODE cur, next;
    if (head→rlink==head)
    {
        cout<<"DELETE IS NOT POSSIBLE, EMPTY"<<endl;
        return head;
    }
    cur=head→rlink;
    next=cur→rlink;
    head→rlink=next;
    next→llink=head;
    cout<<"deleted element "<<cur→info<<endl;
    delete cur;
    return head;
}
```

4.6.4   Delete a node from the rear end

The delete from rear end operation can be explained by the below figure:

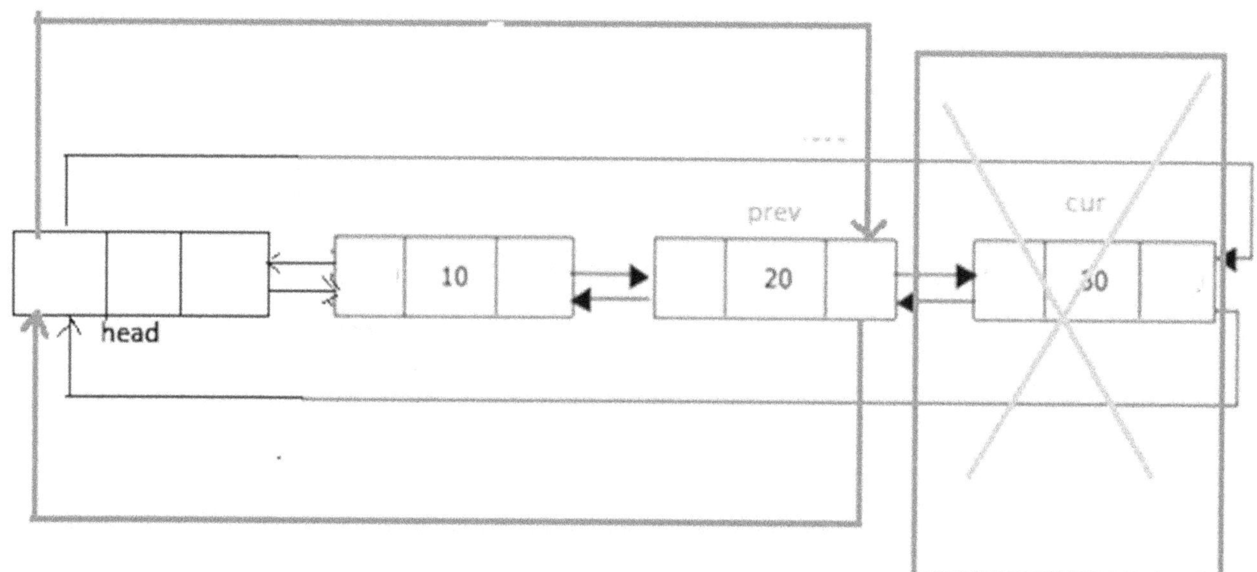

Fig 4.12: Delete a node from the rear end

```cpp
// C++ function to Delete a node from the rear end:
NODE delete_rear (NODE head)
{
    NODE cur, prev;
    if (head→rlink==head)
{

    cout<<"DELETE IS NOT POSSIBLE, EMPTY"<<endl;
    return head;
}

    cur=head→llink;
    prev=cur→llink;
    head→llink=prev;
    prev→rlink=head;
    cout<<"deleted element "<<cur→info<<endl;
    delete cur;
    return head;
}
```

4.6.5   Display the elements of the list

```cpp
// C++ function to Display the elements of the list
void display(NODE head)
{
    NODE cur;
    if(head→rlink==head)
    {
        cout<<"LIST EMPTY"<<endl;
        return;
    }
    cout<<"contents of list are"<<endl;
    cur=head→rlink;
    while(cur≠head)
    {
        cout<<cur→info<<endl;
        cur=cur→rlink;
    }
}
```

4.7 C++ Program to implement the operations of circular doubly linked list.

//Main function

```
#include<iostream>
using namespace std;


//C++ function to create a class Node

class Node
{
    public:
    int info;
    Node *llink;
    Node *rlink;

    public:
        Node(int value)
        {
                info=value;
                llink=NULL;
                rlink=NULL;
        }
};


typedef Node* NODE;


// C++ function to insert a node at the front end of circular Doubly Linked List
NODE insert_front(int ele, NODE head)
{
    NODE newnode, cur;

    newnode=new Node(ele);

    cur=head→rlink;

    head→rlink=newnode;
    newnode→llink=head;
    newnode→rlink=cur;
    cur→llink=newnode;
```

```cpp
        return head;
}

// C++ function to insert a node at the rear end of Doubly Linked List
NODE insert_rear(int ele, NODE head)
{
        NODE newnode, cur;

        newnode=new Node(ele);

        cur=head→llink;

        head→llink=newnode;
newnode→rlink=head;
        newnode→llink=cur;
        cur→rlink=newnode;

        return head;
}

// C++ function to Delete a node from the front end:
 NODE delete_front(NODE head)
{
        NODE cur, next;

        if (head→rlink==head)
        {
                cout<<"DELETE IS NOT POSSIBLE, EMPTY"<<endl;
                return head;
        }

        cur=head→rlink;
        next=cur→rlink;

        head→rlink=next;
        next→llink=head;

        cout<<"deleted element "<<cur→info<<endl;

        delete cur;
        return head;
}
```

```cpp
// C++ function to Delete a node from the rear end:
 NODE delete_rear (NODE head)
{
     NODE cur, prev;

     if (head→rlink==head)
     {
          cout<<"DELETE IS NOT POSSIBLE, EMPTY"<<endl;
          return head;
     }

     cur=head→llink;
     prev=cur→llink;
     head→llink=prev;
     prev→rlink=head;

     cout<<"deleted element "<<cur→info<<endl;
     delete cur;
     return head;
}


// Display the elements of the list

void display(NODE head)
{
     NODE cur;

     if(head→rlink==head)
     {
          cout<<"LIST EMPTY"<<endl;
          return;
     }

     cout<<"contents of list are"<<endl;

     cur=head→rlink;

     while(cur≠head)
     {
          cout<<cur→info<<endl;
          cur=cur→rlink;
     }
```

```cpp
}

//main function
int main()
{
    NODE head;
    int ele,choice,key;
    head=new Node(0);
    head→rlink=head→llink=head;

    for(;;)
      {
            cout<<"1.Display the contents"<<endl<<
                 "2.Add  at the beginning"<<endl<<
                 "3.Add at the end"<<endl<<
                 "4. Delete_front"<<endl<<
                 "5.Delete_rear"<<endl<<
               "6.Exit"<<endl;
            cout<<"Enter your choice: "<<endl;
            cin>>choice;
            switch(choice)
            {
                case 1:
                    display(head);
                    break;
                case 2:
                    cout<<"enter the element to be inserted"<<endl;
                    cin>>ele;
                    head=insert_front(ele,head);
                    break;
                case 3:
                    cout<<"enter the element to be inserted"<<endl;
                    cin>>ele;
                    head=insert_rear(ele,head);
                    break;
                case 4:
                    head=delete_front(head);
                    break;
                case 5:
                    head=delete_rear(head);
                    break;
```

```
                case 6:exit(0);
                default:
                        cout<<"invalid choice"<<endl;
            }
        }
}
Output:
1.Display the contents
2.Add  at the beginning
3.Add at the end
4. Delete_front
5.Delete_rear
6.Exit
Enter your choice:
2
enter the element to be inserted
10
1.Display the contents
2.Add  at the beginning
3.Add at the end
4. Delete_front
5.Delete_rear
6.Exit
Enter your choice:
3
enter the element to be inserted
20
1.Display the contents
2.Add  at the beginning
3.Add at the end
4. Delete_front
5.Delete_rear
6.Exit
Enter your choice:
1
contents of list are
10
20
1.Display the contents
2.Add  at the beginning
3.Add at the end
4. Delete_front
```

```
5.Delete_rear
6.Exit
Enter your choice:
4
deleted element 10
1.Display the contents
2.Add  at the beginning
3.Add at the end
4. Delete_front
5.Delete_rear
6.Exit
Enter your choice:
5
deleted element 20
1.Display the contents
2.Add  at the beginning
3.Add at the end
4. Delete_front
5.Delete_rear
6.Exit
Enter your choice:
1
LIST EMPTY
```

4.8   Advantages and Disadvantages of Circular Doubly Linked List

The advantages and disadvantages of circular linked list are discussed in the following sections:

4.8.1   Advantage of circular linked list

The advantages of circular linked list are:

- Traversing throughout the List is very easy.
- It is time efficient since traversing from one end to the other end requires less time.
- Used in implementation of data structures like queue
- The address or the information related to previous nodes can be obtained easily when compared to singly linked list

Other Applications:

- It is also used by the Operating system to implement algorithms like Round-Robin algorithm.

- Circular Linked List is used in the implementation of data structures like Fibonacci Heap , queues etc,.
- Circular Linked List is used to implement undo function in various applications like word.

4.8.2   Disadvantage of circular linked list

The disadvantages of circular linked list are:

- Circular list are hard to implement when compared to singly linked lists.
- Reversing Circular linked list is tedious job.
- Circular singly linked list might end in infinite loop if not traversed in a proper way.
- Like singly and doubly lists circular linked lists also doesn't support accessing of elements like arrays.

4.9   Advantages and Disadvantages of Doubly Linked List

The advantages and disadvantages of doubly linked list over singly linked list are discussed in the below sections

4.9.1   Advantages of doubly linked list:

- Here,are the advantages of doubly linked list over singly linked list:
- **Traversal Technique:** Doubly linked lists allow traversal in both forward and reverse directions due to the presence of two pointers (llink and rlink) in each node.
- **Deleting a node in Doubly Linked List:** Deleting a node from a doubly linked list is more efficient than in a singly linked list.
- **Insertion and deletion in doubly linked list:** Doubly linked lists enable quick insertion and deletion at both the beginning and end of the list.
- **Enhanced flexibility:** The presence of two pointers in each node provides greater flexibility in manipulating the list.

4.9.2   Disadvantages of Doubly Linked List

Here, are the disadvantages of doubly linked list:

- It requires more memory to store the extra pointers.
- It is a more complex than singly-linked lists.
- Compared to a singly linked list, each node stores an extra pointer which consumes extra memory.
- No random access to elements.

4.9.3   Advantages of Doubly Linked List Over Singly Linked List

Here, are the advantages of doubly linked list over singly linked list:

- It enables efficient reverse traversal.
- They allow for faster deletion of nodes.
- It provides more flexibility in certain algorithms and data structures.
- It is more reflexive and easier to use in certain programming applications.

4.10   List of questions

4. Construct a C program to perform the below functions on doubly linked list without header node:

- createList( )
- isEmpty( )
- size( )
- addFirst( )
- addLast( )
- addAtPosition( )
- addAfterKey( )
- addBeforeKey( )
- removeFirst( )
- removeLast( )
- removeAtPosition( )
- removeAfterKey( )
- removeBeforeKey( )
- display( )
- search( )

5. Construct a C program to perform the below functions on circular doubly linked list without header node:

- createList( )
- isEmpty( )
- size( )
- addFirst( )
- addLast( )
- addAtPosition( )
- addAfterKey( )
- addBeforeKey( )
- removeFirst( )

- removeLast( )
- removeAtPosition( )
- removeAfterKey( )
- removeBeforeKey( )
- display( )
- search( )

6. Construct a C program to perform the below functions on circular doubly linked List with header node:

- createList( )
- isEmpty( )
- size( )
- addFirst( )
- addLast( )
- addAtPosition( )
- addAfterKey( )
- addBeforeKey( )
- removeFirst( )
- removeLast( )
- removeAtPosition( )
- removeAfterKey( )
- removeBeforeKey( )
- display( )
- search( )

7. Construct a C program to perform the below functions on doubly linked List with header node:

- createList( )
- isEmpty( )
- size( )
- addFirst( )
- addLast( )
- addAtPosition( )
- addAfterKey( )
- addBeforeKey( )
- removeFirst( )
- removeLast( )

- removeAtPosition( )
- removeAfterKey( )
- removeBeforeKey( )
- display( )
- search( )

CHAPTER - 5

Chapter 5

Stacks and Queues

Introduction

The stacks and queues are the linear data structures that follows LIFO and FIFO principles. The stack has wide range of applications in implementing recursion, evaluation of expressions, conversion of expressions and so on. The queue data structure is also used in various scheduling algorithms. The stacks and queues can be implemented using arrays and linked lists, and they are abstract data types.

Structure

The chapter will cover the following topics:

- Stacks

  - Definition
  - Stack operations
  - Array Representation of Stacks
  - Stack Applications:
  - Polish Notations
  - Infix to Postfix conversion
  - Evaluation of postfix expression

- Queues

  - Definition
  - Array Representation
  - Queue operations
  - Circular Queues
  - Programming Examples.

Objectives

After reading this chapter, the reader can implement stack and queue data structures using arrays and linked lists. Application of stacks, along with solved problems and executed programs, are discussed in the chapter. The implementation of different types of queues is also given in this book. All the programs are thoroughly tested and debugged.

5.1 Stacks

A Stack is a special type of data structure where elements are inserted in **Last In First Out (LIFO)** or **First In Last Out (FILO)** order.

LIFO – The last element to be inserted is the first element to be deleted.

FILO – The first element to be inserted is the last element to be deleted.

The elements are inserted from one end and the elements are deleted from the same end. The end from which elements are inserted or deleted is called as top of the stack.

5.2 Implementing push, pop and display operations in stack

The various operations that can be performed on stack are as follows:

Push (Inserting an element on the top of stack)

Pop (Deleting an element from the top of the stack)

Display (Display elements of stack)

5.2.1 Push operation

Inserting an element into the stack is called push operation.

Only one item can be inserted at a time and that element should be inserted only from the top of the stack since element are inserted or deleted from only one end called top in the stack.

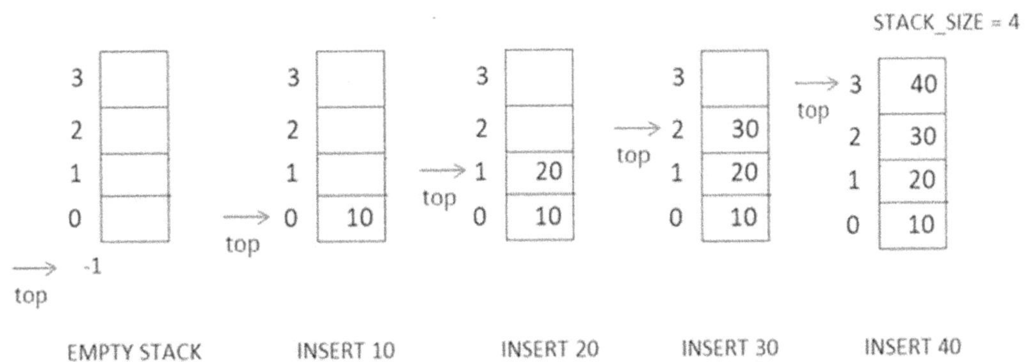

Fig 5.1: Pictorial representation of Push operation

Stack overflow

When elements are being inserted, there are chances of stack being full. Once the stack is full, it is not possible to insert any element. Trying to insert an element even when the stack is full results in an overflow of the stack.

The condition where the stack is full and we cannot insert an element further into the stack is called **stack overflow**.

Example:

Consider the stack shown in *Fig 5.2* above with STACK_SIZE 4. We can insert a maximum of 4 elements. After inserting 10, 20, 30, 40 there is no space to insert the 5th element. We say that the stack is full. This condition is called overflow of stack.

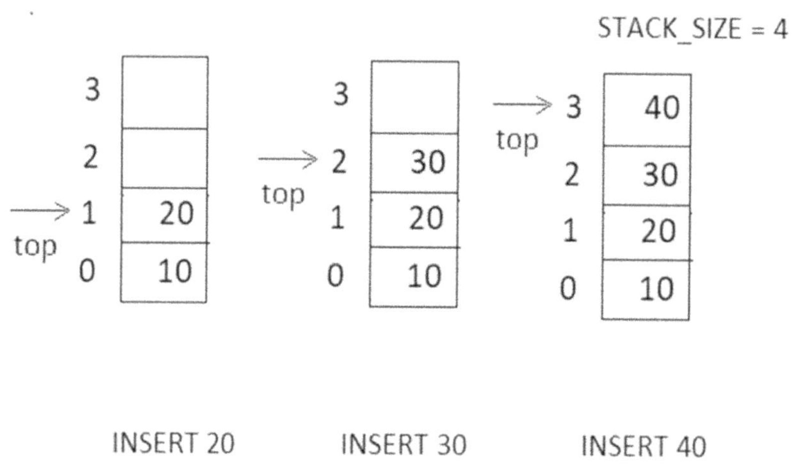

Fig 5.2: Pictorial representation of stack overflow

To insert the element into the stack, consider the *Fig 5.2*. We know that 30 has to be inserted at top =2. To insert the next element 40, we have to increment top by 1. This can be done using the statement:

```
top=top+1;
```

Now, we can insert item into the stack using the statement:

```
s[top]=ele;
```

We cannot insert any element into the stack when the stack is full. In such situations, we can display an appropriate message as shown below:

```
if(top==STACK_SIZE - 1)
{
        cout<<"Stack Overflow"<<endl;
        return;
}
```

5.2.2 C++ function to insert element into stack

```
void push(Stacks *s,int ele)
{
      if(s→top==STACK_SIZE-1)
      {
            cout<<"Stack Overflow"<<endl;
            return;
      }

      (s→top)++;
      s→s[s→top]=ele;


}
```

5.2.3 Pop operation

Deleting an element from the stack is called pop operation. Only one element can be deleted at a time and element has to be deleted only from the top of the stack.

Stack underflow

When elements are being deleted, we may get stack underflow.

When elements are being deleted, there are chances of the stack being empty. When a stack is empty, it is not possible to delete any element. Trying to delete an element from an empty stack results in **stack underflow.**

Example:

After deleting 10, 20, 30, 40, there are no elements in the stack, and the stack is empty. Deleting an element from this empty stack results in **stack underflow.**

To delete an element from the top of the stack, decrement top by one as shown below:

```
top = top-1;
```

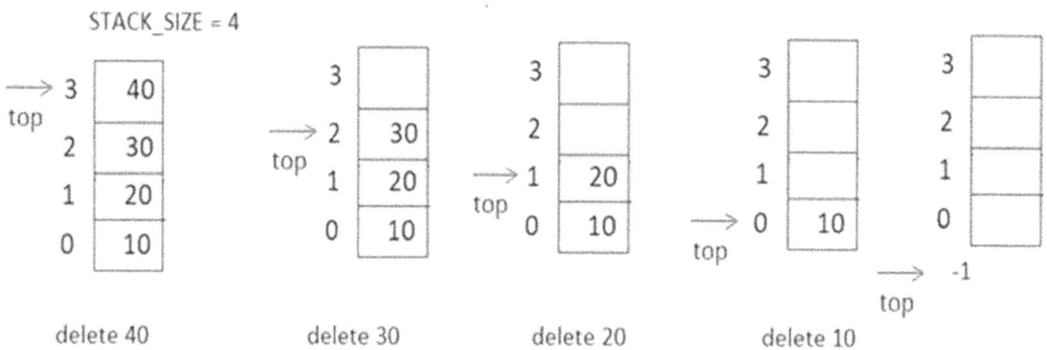

Fig 5.3: Pictorial representation of pop operation

When top=-1, the stack is empty and we cannot delete elements . This condition is given using:

```
if(top==- 1)
{
cout<<"Stack Underflow"<<endl;
return;
}
```

5.2.4   C++ function to delete an element into stack

```
void pop(Stacks *s)
{
     if(s→top==-1)
     {
          cout<<"Stack Underflow"<<endl;
          return;
     }

     cout<<"element deleted is "<< s→s[s→top];
     s→top--;

}
```

5.2.5   Display operation

If the stack is not empty, the elements have to be displayed one after the other. If no elements are present, then a suitable error message is displayed.

Design:

Assume that the stack contains three elements as shown below:

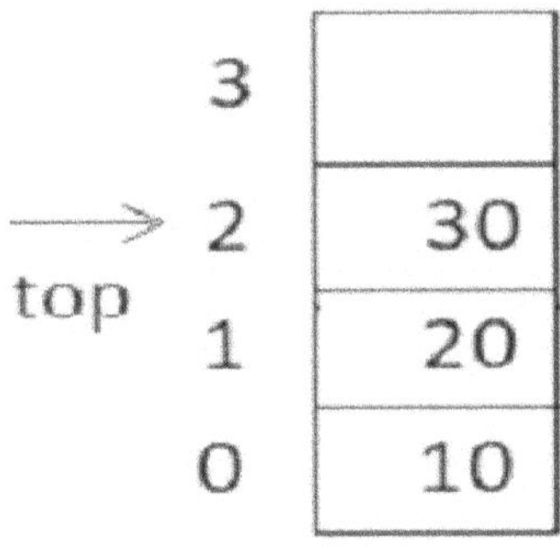

Fig 5.4: *Pictorial representation of display operation*

```
The value of i changes from 0 to top.
i.e
cout<<s[0];                     10
cout<<s[1];                     20
cout<<s[2];                     30

cout<<s[i];              here i= 0 to 2 i.e
                         i=0 to top
```

5.2.6   C++ function to display elements of stack

```cpp
void display(Stacks *s)
{
    int i;

    if(s→top==-1)
    {
        cout<<"Stack Empty"<<endl;
        return;
    }

    cout<<"Contents of stack are"<<endl;

    for(i=0;i≤s→top;i++)
    {
```

```
        cout<<s→s[i]<<endl;
    }
}
```

5.2.7   Push and Pop Algorithm:

<table>
<tr><td>

Push(item)

If top == size-1 then

Print 'Stack overflow'

Exit

Else

top=top+1

A[top]=item

Exit

Pop()

If top==-1 then

Print 'stack underflow'

Exit

Else

Item=a[top]

top = top-1

Exit

</td><td>

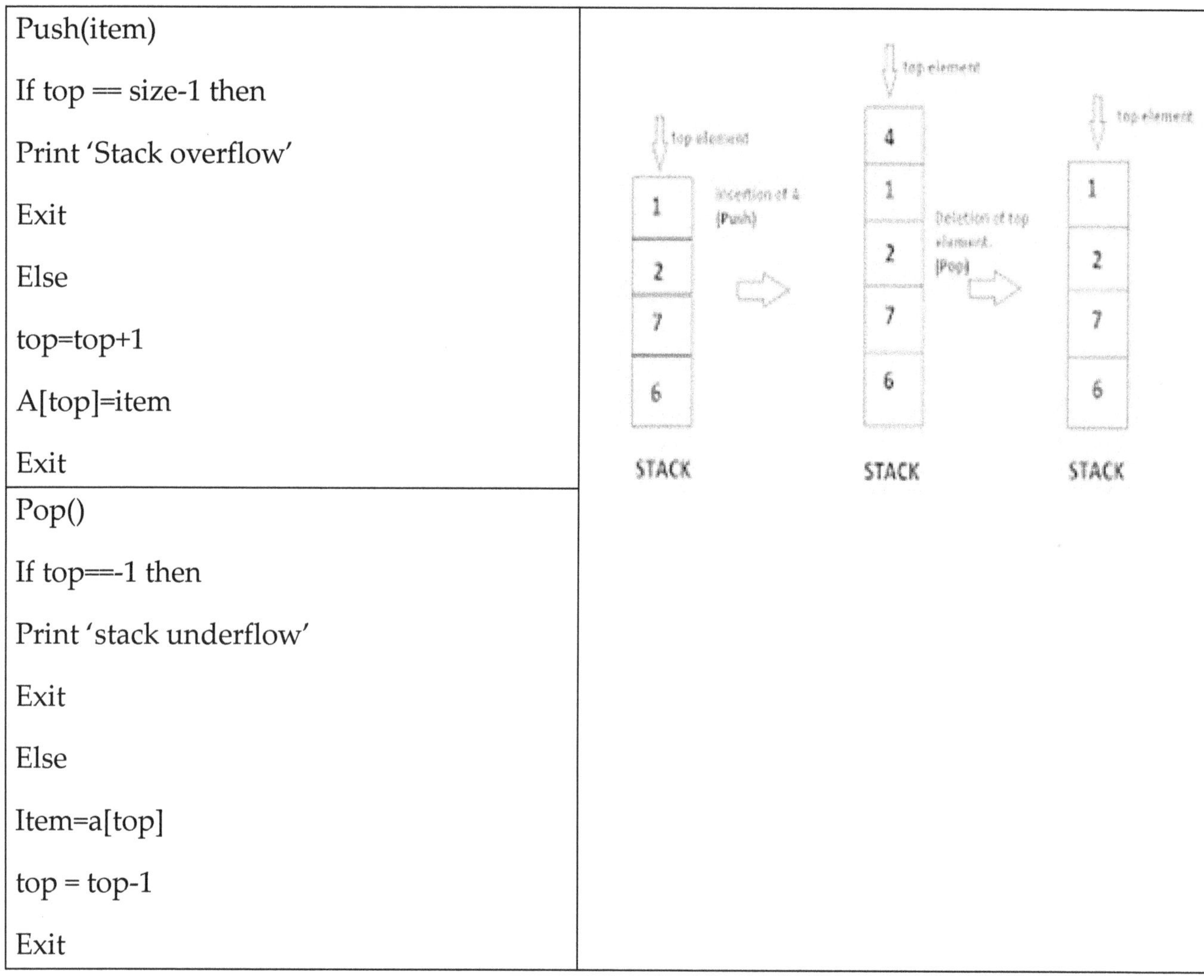

</td></tr>
</table>

Peek()
 	
  If top==-1 then
 	
Print 'stack underflow'
 	
Exit
 	
Else
 	
Print a[top]
	top element = 60
	
	5 60
	4 50
	3 40
	2 30
	1 20
	0 10

Display()
 	
If top==-1 then
 	
Print 'stack underflow'
 	
Exit
 	
Else
 	
For i from top to 0
 	
  Print a[i]
	For above figure output will be
	
	60
	
	50
	
	40
	
	30
	
	20
	
	10

NOTE: The other operations on stack are discussed at the end of this chapter

5.3   Stack implementation using arrays

```cpp
#include<iostream>
using namespace std;
#define STACK_SIZE 5

class Stacks
{
    public:
    int top;
    int s[10];

    public:
    Stacks()
    {
```

```cpp
            top=-1;
        }
};


//C++ function to insert element into stack;
void push(Stacks *s,int ele)
{
        if(s→top==STACK_SIZE-1)
        {
                cout<<"Stack Overflow"<<endl;
                return;
        }


        (s→top)++;
        s→s[s→top]=ele;

}
//C++ function to delete an element into stack;
void pop(Stacks *s)
{
        if(s→top==-1)
        {
                cout<<"Stack Underflow"<<endl;
                return;
        }

        cout<<"element deleted is "<< s→s[s→top];
        s→top--;

}



//C++ function to display elements of stack;
void display(Stacks *s)
{
    int i;

        if(s→top==-1)
        {
                cout<<"Stack Empty"<<endl;
                return;
        }
```

```cpp
        cout<<"Contents of stack are"<<endl;

        for(i=0;i<=s->top;i++)
        {
                cout<<s->s[i]<<endl;
        }
}
int main()
{

        Stacks *st=new Stacks();
        int choice,ele;
        for(;;)
        {
                cout<<"1. Push"<<endl<<" 2. Pop"<<endl<<" 3. Display"<<endl<<"
4.Exit"<<endl;
                cout<<"enter the choice"<<endl;
                cin>>choice;
                switch(choice)
                {
                        case 1: cout<<"enter element to be inserted"<<endl;
                                cin>>ele;
                                push(st,ele);
                                break;
                        case 2: pop(st);
                                break;
                        case 3: display(st);
                                break;
                        default: exit(0);
                }
        }
        return 0;
}
```

Output:

```
1.Push (INSERT)  2. Pop (DELETE)  3. Display  4.Exit (STOP)
enter the choice
1
enter element to be inserted
10
```

```
1.Push (INSERT)  2. Pop (DELETE)  3. Display  4.Exit (STOP)
enter the choice
1
enter element to be inserted
20

1.Push (INSERT)  2. Pop (DELETE)  3. Display  4.Exit (STOP)
enter the choice
1
enter element to be inserted
30

1.Push (INSERT)  2. Pop (DELETE)  3. Display  4.Exit (STOP)
enter the choice
1
enter element to be inserted
40

1.Push (INSERT)  2. Pop (DELETE)  3. Display  4.Exit (STOP)
enter the choice
1
enter element to be inserted
50

1.Push (INSERT)  2. Pop (DELETE)  3. Display  4.Exit (STOP)
enter the choice
1
enter element to be inserted
60
Stack Overflow

1.Push (INSERT)  2. Pop (DELETE)  3. Display  4.Exit (STOP)
enter the choice
3
Contents of stack are
50
40
30
20
10
```

```
1.Push (INSERT)  2. Pop (DELETE)  3. Display  4.Exit (STOP)
enter the choice
2
element deleted is 50

1.Push (INSERT)  2. Pop (DELETE)  3. Display  4.Exit (STOP)
enter the choice
2
element deleted is 40

1.Push (INSERT)  2. Pop (DELETE)  3. Display  4.Exit (STOP)
enter the choice
2
element deleted is 30

1.Push (INSERT)  2. Pop (DELETE)  3. Display  4.Exit (STOP)
enter the choice
2
element deleted is 20

1.Push (INSERT)  2. Pop (DELETE)  3. Display  4.Exit (STOP)
enter the choice
2
element deleted is 10

1.Push (INSERT)  2. Pop (DELETE)  3. Display  4.Exit (STOP)
enter the choice
2
Stack underflow


1.Push (INSERT)  2. Pop (DELETE)  3. Display  4.Exit (STOP)
enter the choice
3
Stack Empty
```

5.4   Stack applications

The applications of stack are as discussed below:

- Conversion of expressions: The expressions can be converted from one form to another (infix to postfix, infix to prefix, prefix to postfix and so on) using stack data structure.

- Evaluation of expressions: An arithmetic expression either in the prefix or postfix form can be evaluated using stack.
- Recursion: Recursive functions are the functions which call itself. Recursive function uses stack data structure.
- Other applications: Some of the problems like string palindrome, balanced parenthesis can be solved using stack.

5.5   Polish notations

This type of notation was introduced by the Polish mathematician *Lukasiewicz*. Polish Notation in data structure tells us about different ways to write an arithmetic expression.

The polish notations can be classified into three types:

- **Infix polish notation or infix expression:**

In an expression, if an operator is in between two operands, the expression is called infix expression also called as infix polish notation. The infix expression can be either parenthesized or un parenthesized.

Example:

a+b is an un parenthesized infix expression.

(a+b) is a parenthesized infix expression.

- **Postfix polish notation or postfix expression:**

In an expression, if an operator follows or succeeds operands, the expression is called Postfix polish notation or postfix expression. The postfix expression is always unparenthesized.

Example:

ab+ is a postfix expression.

- **Prefix polish notation or prefix expression:**

In an expression, if an operator precedes operands, the expression is called Prefix polish notation or prefix expression. The prefix expression is always unparenthesized.

Example:

+ab is a prefix expression.

5.6   Infix to postfix conversion

The algorithm to convert infix expression to postfix expression is discussed as follows:

5.6.1   Algorithm

1. Scan the infix expression from left to right and push ('#') on stack.
2. If the scanned character is an operand, then put it in result string or print it into output.
3. If the scanned character is a '(', push it to the stack.
4. If the scanned character is a ')', pop the stack and and output it until a '(' is encountered, and discard both the parenthesis.(i.e one extra pop to remove '(' , but dont add it to result string).
5. Else (if operator is scanned).

   .....**5.1** If the precedence of the scanned operator is greater than the precedence of the operator on the top of stack then push it.

   .....**5.2** Else, pop all the operators from the stack which are greater than or equal to in precedence than that of the scanned operator. After doing that push the scanned operator to the stack.6. Repeat *Steps 2-6* until infix expression is scanned.7. Print the output.

6. Pop and output from the stack until # value on stack.

5.6.2   Examples

- **Convert infix expression A*B-(C+D)+E to postfix expression:**

Solution:

Input Symbol	Stack	Postfix Expression
A	EMPTY STACK	A
*	*	A
B	*	AB
-	-	AB*
(	-(	AB*
C	-(	AB*C
+	-(+	AB*C
D	-(+	AB*CD
)	-	AB*CD+
+	+	AB*CD+-
E	+	AB*CD+-E
EOI	EMPTY STACK	AB*CD+-E+

Table 4.2:

Postfix expression: AB*CD+-E+

- **Convert A^B*C/(D*E-F) to postfix expression.**

Solution:

Input symbol	Stack	Postfix expression
A	EMPTY STACK	A
^	^	A
B	^	AB
*	*	AB^
C	*	AB^C
/	/	AB^C*
(	/(	AB^C*
D	/(	AB^C*D
*	/(*	AB^C*D
E	/(*	AB^C*DE
-	/(-	AB^C*DE*
F	/(-	AB^C*DE*F
)	/	AB^C*DE*F-
EOI	EMPTY STACK	AB^C*DE*F-/

Table 4.2:

Postfix expression: AB^C*DE*F-/

- **Convert infix expression 8*(5^4+2)-6^2/(5*3) to postfix expression**

Solution:

Input symbol	Stack	Postfix expression
8	Empty stack	8
*	*	8
(	*(	8
5	*(	85
^	*(^	85
4	*(^	854
+	*(+	854^
2	*(+	854^2
)	*	854^2+
-	-	854^2+*
6	-	854^2+*6

^	-^	854^2+*6
2	-^	854^2+*62
/	-/	854^2+*62^
(	-/(	854^2+*62^
9	-/(	854^2+*62^9
*	-/(*	854^2+*62^9
3	-/(*	854^2+*62^93
)	-/	854^2+*62^93*
EOI	EMPTY STACK	854^2+*62^93*/-

Table 4.3:

Postfix expression: 854^2+*62^93*/-

- **Convert infix expression A+B/(C*D^E) -F*G^H to postfix expression.**

Solution:

Input symbol	Stack	Postfix expression
A	EMPTY STACK	A
+	+	A
B	+	AB
/	+/	AB
(	+/(	AB
C	+/(	ABC
*	+/(*	ABC
D	+/(*	ABCD
^	+/(*^	ABCD
E	+/(*^	ABCDE
)	+/(*^	ABCDE^*
-	-	ABCDE^*/+
F	-	ABCDE^*/+F
*	-*	ABCDE^*/+F
G	-*	ABCDE^*/+FG
^	-*^	ABCDE^*/+FG
H	-*^	ABCDE^*/+FGH
EOI	EMPTY STACK	ABCDE^*/+FGH^*-

Table 4.4:

Postfix expression: ABCDE^*/+FGH^*-

5.7   C++ Program to convert infix to postfix

```cpp
#include<iostream>
using namespace std;
#include<string.h>
#include <ctype.h>
#define SIZE 50                                /* Size of Stack */

char s[SIZE];
int top=-1;                              /* Global declarations */

push(char elem)
{                                /* Function for PUSH operation */
    s[++top]=elem;
}
char pop()
{                                 /* Function for POP operation */
    return(s[top--]);
}

int pr(char elem)                   /* Function for precedence */
{
    switch(elem)
    {
        case '#': return 0;
        case '(': return 1;
        case '+':
        case '-': return 2;
        case '*':
        case '/': return 3;
        case '$':
        case '^': return 4;
    }
}

main()
{
    char infix[50],pofix[50],ch,elem;
    int i=0,k=0;
```

```cpp
cout<<"\n\nRead the Infix Expression ? "<<endl;
cin>>infix;

push('#');

while( (ch=infix[i++]) != '\0')
{
    if(ch=='(')                      /* For left parentheses */
        push(ch);

    else if(isalnum(ch))             /* For operand */
        pofix[k++]=ch;

    else if(ch==')')                 /* For Right parentheses */
    {
        while( s[top] != '(' )
            pofix[k++]=pop();
        elem=pop();                  /* Remove ( */
    }

    else
    {                                /* For Operator */
        while( pr(s[top]) >= pr(ch) )
            pofix[k++]=pop();
        push(ch);
    }
}
        while(s[top] != '#')         /* Pop from stack till empty */
        pofix[k++]=pop();

    pofix[k]='\0';                   /* Make pofx as valid string */

    cout<<"\n\nGiven Infix Expn:"<<infix<<endl<<"postfix expression
is"<<pofix<<endl;

}
```

Output:

```
Read the Infix Expression
A+B/(C*D^E) -F*G^H
Given Infix Expn: A+B/(C*D^E) -F*G^H
Postfix Expn: ABCDE^*/+FGH^*-
```

5.8   Postfix evaluation

The Postfix notation is used to represent algebraic expressions. The expressions written in postfix form are evaluated faster compared to infix notation as parenthesis are not required in postfix.

5.9   Algorithm for evaluation of postfix expressions

Create a stack to store operands (or values).

Scan the given expression and do following for every scanned element.

If the element is a number, push it into the stack.

If the element is an operator, pop operands for the operator from stack. Evaluate the operator and push the result back to the stack

When the expression is ended, the number in the stack is the final answer

5.10   Examples

Evaluate the expression 6 2 3 + - 3 8 2 / +*2$3+

Solution:

Symbol	Opnd 1	Opnd 2	value	Stack
6				6
2				6,2
3				6,2,3
+	2	3	5	6,5
-	6	5	1	1
3	6	5	1	1,3
8	6	5	1	1,3,8
2	6	5	1	1,3,8,2
/	8	2	4	1,3,4
+	3	4	7	1,7

Symbol	Opnd 1	Opnd 2	value	Stack
*	1	7	7	7
2	1	7	7	7,2
$	7	2	49	49
3	7	2	49	49,3
+	49	3	52	52

Table 4.5

Result after evaluation: 52

Evaluate the expression 7532^*922^-/+64*+

Solution:

Symbol	Operand 1	Operand 2	Value	Stack
7				7
5				7,5
3				7,5,3
2				7,5,3,2
^	3	2	9	7,5,9
*	5	9	45	7,45
9				7,45,9
2				7,45,9,2
2				7,45,9,2,2
^	2	2	4	7,45,9,4
-	9	4	5	7,45,5
/	45	5	9	7,9
+	7	9	16	16
6				16,6
4				16,6,4
*	6	4	24	16,24
+	16	24	40	40

Table 4.6

Result after evaluation:40

Evaluate the expression 632-5*+1^7+

Solution:

Symbol	Operand 1	Operand 2	Value	Stack
6				6
3				6,3
2				6,3,2
-	3	2	1	6,1
5				6,1,5
*	1	5	5	6,5
+	6	5	11	11
1				11,1
^	11	1	11	11
7				11,7
+	11	7	18	18

Table 4.7

Result after evaluation :18

5.11   C++ Program to evaluate postfix expression:

```cpp
#include<iostream>
using namespace std;
#include <ctype.h>
#define SIZE 50                              /* Size of Stack */

int s[SIZE];
int top= -1;                                 /* Global declarations */

void push(int elem)           /* Function FOR PUSH operation */
{
        s[++top]=elem;
}
int pop()                     /* Function FOR POP operation */
{
        return(s[top--]);
}
main()
{
        char pofix[50],ch;
```

```cpp
        int i=0,op1,op2;
        cout<<"Read the Postfix Expression ? "<<endl;
        cin>>pofix;
        while( (ch=pofix[i++]) ≠ '\0')
        {
                if(isdigit(ch))
                        push(ch-'0'); /* Push the operand */
                else
                {                       /*pop two  operands */
                        op2=pop();
                        op1=pop();
                        switch(ch)
                        {
                            case '+': push(op1+op2);
                                              break;
                                case '-':  push(op1-op2);
                                              break;
                                case '*': push(op1*op2);
                                              break;
                                case '/':  push(op1/op2);
                                              break;


                        }
                }
        }
        cout<<"Given Postfix Expn: "<<endl<<pofix;
        cout<<"Result after Evaluation: "<<endl<<s[top];


}
```

Output:

```
Read the Postfix Expression
63+
Given Postfix Expn:
63+
Result after Evaluation:9
```

5.12   Queues

A queue is a FIFO data structure.It is a special type of data structure where elements are inserted from one end and deleted from the other end.

The end from which new elements are added is called the rear end and end from which the elements are deleted is called front end. The first element inserted is the first element to go out of the queue.

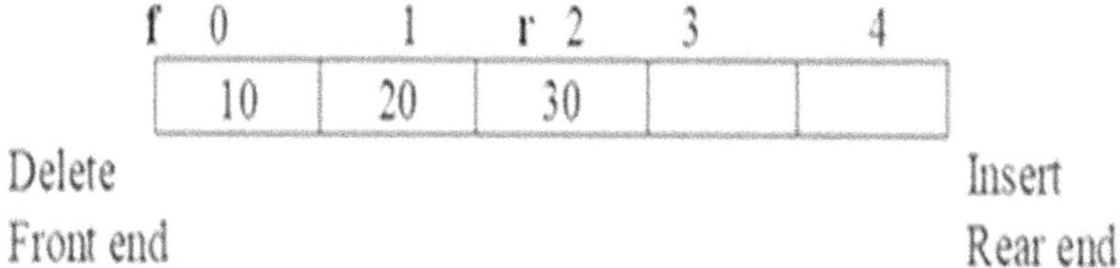

Fig 5.5: Pictorial Representation of Queue

f=front end , the end from where elements are deleted

r=rear end, the end from where elements are inserted

QUEUE_SIZE=5 which is the maximum size of queue

5.13   Operations on queue

The operations which can be performed on Queue (of any type) are as follows:

Enqueue: Inserting elements into the queue is called enqueue operation

Dequeue: Deleting elements from the queue is called dequeue operation

Display: Displaying queue elements is called display operation.

5.14   Types of queues

Based on the operations performed and the method of inserting elements in the queue, the queues are classified into following types:

- Queue (ordinary queue)
- Circular queue
- Double ended queue
- Priority queue

5.15 Queue (ordinary queue)

The type of queue where insertion happens at one end called rear end and deletion happens at the other end called front end is called ordinary queue.

Operation on queues are as follows:

- Insert an element into queue also called as enqueue operation
- Delete an element from queue also called as dequeue operation
- Display the contents of queue also called as display operation

5.15.1 Enqueue

Inserting elements into the queue is called enqueue.

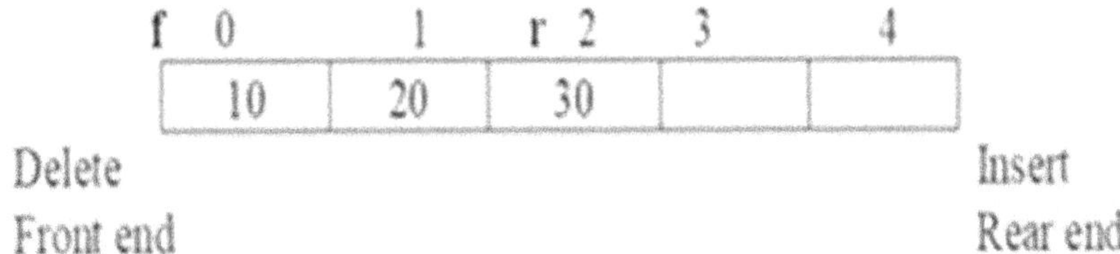

Fig 5.6 (a): Before insert

Now, if we have to insert an element 40, the element has to be inserted at r=3. For this to happen, we have to increment r by 1. This can be achieved using the statement:

`r=r+1;`

This is followed by copying element "ele" to q[r] using the following statement:

`q[r] = ele;`

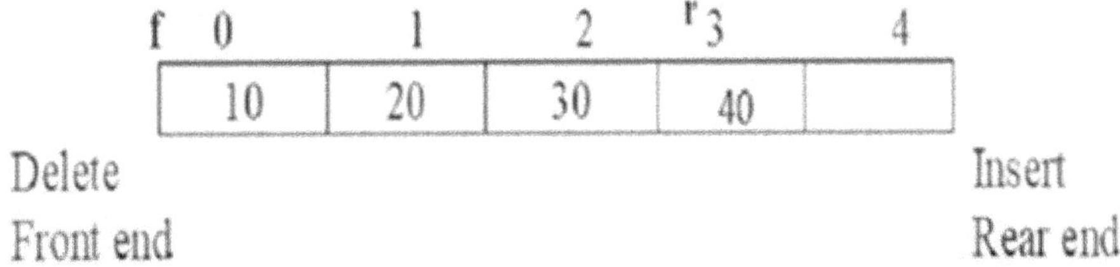

Fig 5.6 (b): After Inserting 40

Now, 50 can be inserted at r=4 using the above two statements.

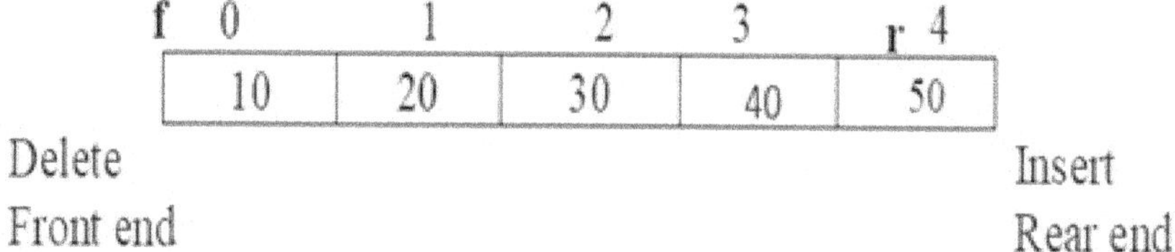

Fig 5.6 (c): After Inserting 50

Now if we try insert 60 in the above queue, 60 cannot be inserted since **r** has already reached QUEUE_SIZE -1(QUEUE_SIZE=5). In such situations, we have to display appropriate message as follows:

```
if (q→r==QUEUE_SIZE -1)
{
    cout<<"QUEUE overflow"<<endl;
    return;
}
```

The element can be inserted into the queue only if the above condition fails:

5.15.2   C++ function to insert an element

```
void insert_rear(Queues q)
{
    if (q→r==QUEUE_SIZE -1)
    {
        cout<<"QUEUE overflow"<<endl;
        return;
    }
    q→r=q→r+1;
    q→q[q→r]=ele;

}
```

5.15.3 Dequeue

Deleting elements from the queue is called dequeue.

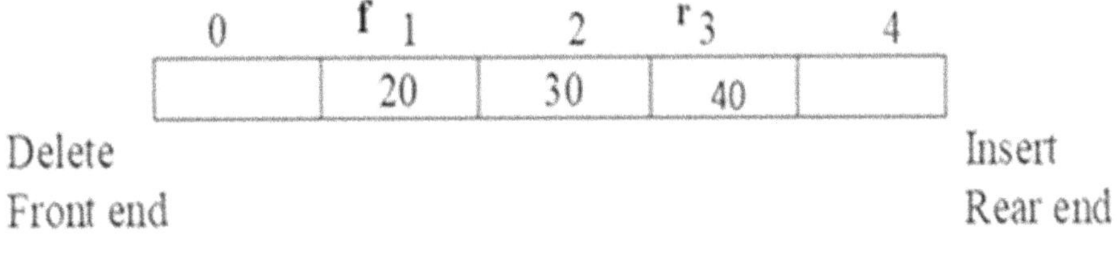

Fig 5.7(a) : *After deleting 1ˢᵗ element*

(a)

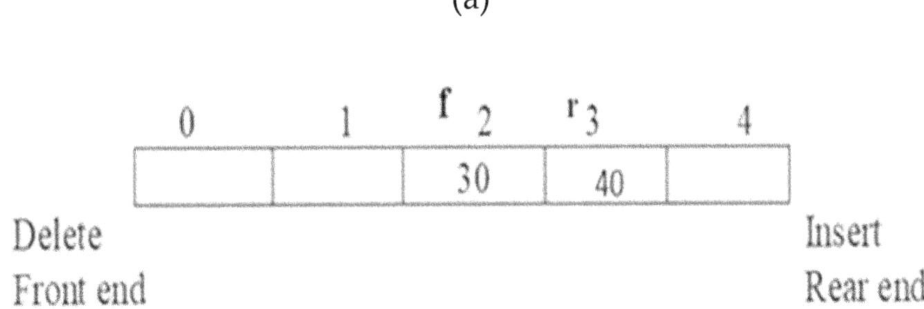

Fig 5.7(b): *After deleting 2ⁿᵈ element*

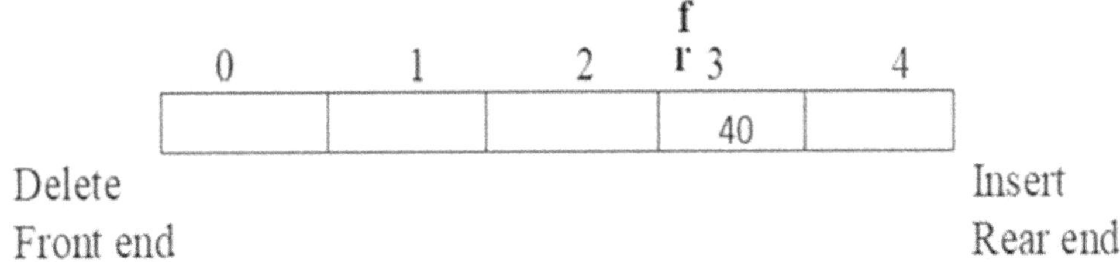

Fig 5.7(c): *After deleting 3ʳᵈ element*

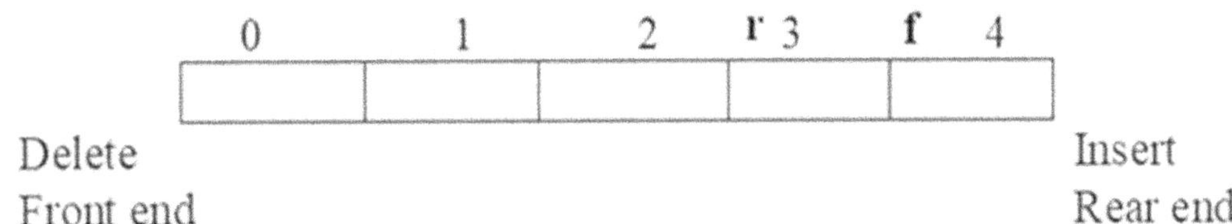

Fig 5.7(d): *After deleting 4ᵗʰ element*

Element has to be deleted from the front end of the queue which can be achieved by incrementing f by one. From the above figure we can see that rear insertion is not possible even if there is space in the queue. This condition is called queue underflow, that is, when f will become greater than r, elements cannot be deleted.

```
if (q→f>q→r)
    {
        cout<<"QUEUE underflow"<<endl;
        return;
    }
```

Deletion can be achieved by incrementing f by one as shown below:
```
q→f=q→f+1;
```
Before deleting, we try to display the deleted element as shown below:
```
cout<<"Item deleted = "<<q→q[q→f];
```
The above two statements can be written using the single statement:
```
Cout<<"Item deleted "<<q→q[q→f++]<<endl;
```

5.15.4   C++ function to delete an element from queue

```
void delete_front(Queues *q)
{
    if (q→f>q→r)
    {
        cout<<"QUEUE underflow"<<endl;
        return;
    }
    cout<<"Item deleted = "<<q→q[q→f];
    q→f=q→f+1;
    if(q→f>q→r) q→f=0,q→r=-1;
```

5.15.5   Display queue elements

Displaying queue elements is display operation.

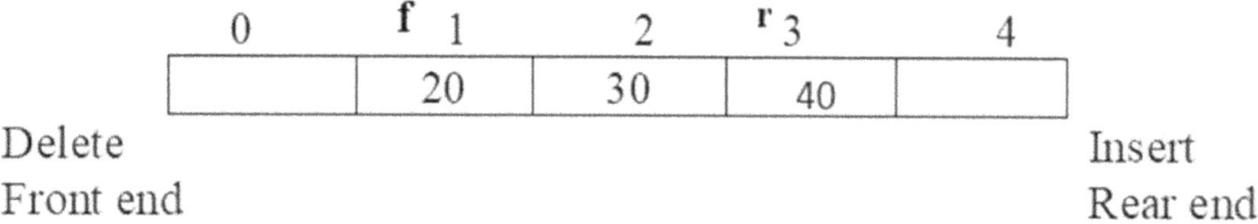

Fig 5.8: Display queue element

Consider the queue where 4 elements are inserted and the 1ˢᵗ element has been deleted:

```c
printf("%d\n",q[1]);
printf("%d\n",q[2]);
printf("%d\n",q[3]);


In general, we can use printf("%d\n",q[i]);
Where i=1 to 3
                        i=f to r
```

5.15.6   C++ function to display the queue elements

```cpp
void display(Queues q)
{
      int i;

      if(q.f>q.r)
      {
            cout<<"Queue is empty"<<endl;
            return;
      }

      cout<<"contents of queue are"<<endl;

      for(i=q.f;i≤q.r;i++)
      {
            cout<<endl<<q.q[i];
      }
}
```

5.16   C++ Program to implement operations on queues

```cpp
#include<iostream>
using namespace std;
#define QUEUE_SIZE 5

class Queues
{
      public:
      int f, r, q[10], ele;
```

```cpp
        Queues()
        {
                f=0;
                r=-1;
        }

};


//C++ function to insert an element:
void insert_rear(Queues *q, int ele)
{
        if (q→r==QUEUE_SIZE -1)
        {
                cout<<"QUEUE overflow"<<endl;
                return;
        }
        q→r=q→r+1;
        q→q[q→r]=ele;

}


// C++ function to delete an element from queue:
void delete_front(Queues *q)
{
        if (q→f>q→r)
        {
                cout<<"QUEUE underflow"<<endl;
                return;
        }
        cout<<"Item deleted = "<<q→q[q→f];
        q→f=q→f+1;
        if(q→f>q→r) q→f=0,q→r=-1;

}
//C++ function to display the queue elements:
void display(Queues q)
{
        int i;

        if(q.f>q.r)
        {
                cout<<"Queue is empty"<<endl;
```

```cpp
		return;
	}

	cout<<"contents of queue are"<<endl;

	for(i=q.f;i≤q.r;i++)
	{
		cout<<endl<<q.q[i];
	}
}


//main function
int main()
{
	Queues que;
	int choice,ele;
	for(;;)
	{
		cout<<"1. Enqueue2. Dequeue 3. Display 4. Exit"<<endl;
		cout<<"enter the choice"<<endl;
		cin>>choice;

		switch(choice)
		{
			case 1: cout<<"enter element to be inserted"<<endl;
				cin>>ele;
				insert_rear(&que,ele);
				break;
			case 2: delete_front(&que);
				break;
			case 3: display(que);
				break;
			default: exit(0);
		}
	}
}
```

Output:

```
     1. Enqueue2. Dequeue 3. Display 4. Exit (STOP)
enter the choice
1
enter element to be inserted
10

     1. Enqueue2. Dequeue 3. Display 4. Exit (STOP)
enter the choice
1
enter element to be inserted
20

     1. Enqueue2. Dequeue 3. Display 4. Exit (STOP)
enter the choice
1
enter element to be inserted
30

     1. Enqueue2. Dequeue 3. Display 4. Exit (STOP)
enter the choice
1
enter element to be inserted
40

     1. Enqueue2. Dequeue 3. Display 4. Exit (STOP)
enter the choice
1
enter element to be inserted
50

     1. Enqueue2. Dequeue 3. Display 4. Exit (STOP)
enter the choice
1
enter element to be inserted
60
QUEUE Overflow

     1. Enqueue2. Dequeue 3. Display 4. Exit (STOP)
enter the choice
3
```

```
Contents of stack are
10
20
30
40
50

        1. Enqueue2. Dequeue 3. Display 4. Exit (STOP)
enter the choice
2
element deleted is 10

        1. Enqueue2. Dequeue 3. Display 4. Exit (STOP)
enter the choice
2
element deleted is 20

        1. Enqueue2. Dequeue 3. Display 4. Exit (STOP)
enter the choice
2
element deleted is 30

        1. Enqueue2. Dequeue 3. Display 4. Exit (STOP)
enter the choice
2
element deleted is 40

        1. Enqueue2. Dequeue 3. Display 4. Exit (STOP)
enter the choice
2
element deleted is 50

        1. Enqueue2. Dequeue 3. Display 4. Exit (STOP)
enter the choice
2
QUEUE underflow

        1. Enqueue2. Dequeue 3. Display 4. Exit (STOP)
enter the choice
3
QUEUE Empty
```

5.17   Disadvantage of queue

The disadvantage of queue can be understood by the following scenario:

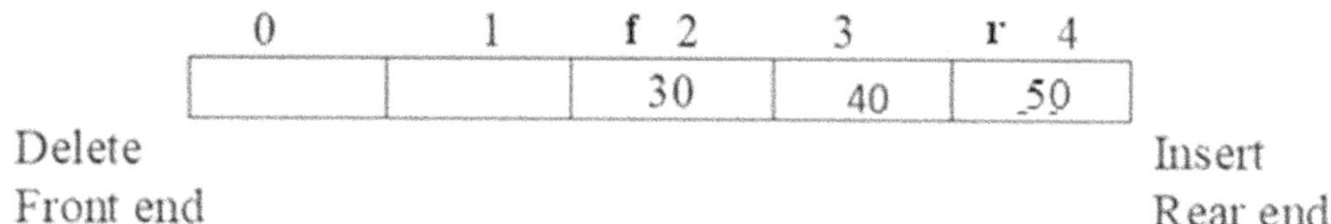

Fig 5.9: Pictorial representation Of queue

Consider the queue shown above. Imagine that 10, 20, 30, 40, 50 are inserted initially into the queue from the rear end and the first two elements 10 and 20 are deleted from the queue. Now, if we try to insert element into queue from the rear end, we get the message as "queue overflow".

Rear insertion is not possible even if the space is available at the front end, which is a disadvantage. This can be overcome using circular queue.

5.18   Circular queues

In the circular queue, the elements of a given queue are stored such that the end of the queue is followed by the front of queue.

The pictorial representation of empty queue and queue with three elements are shown below:

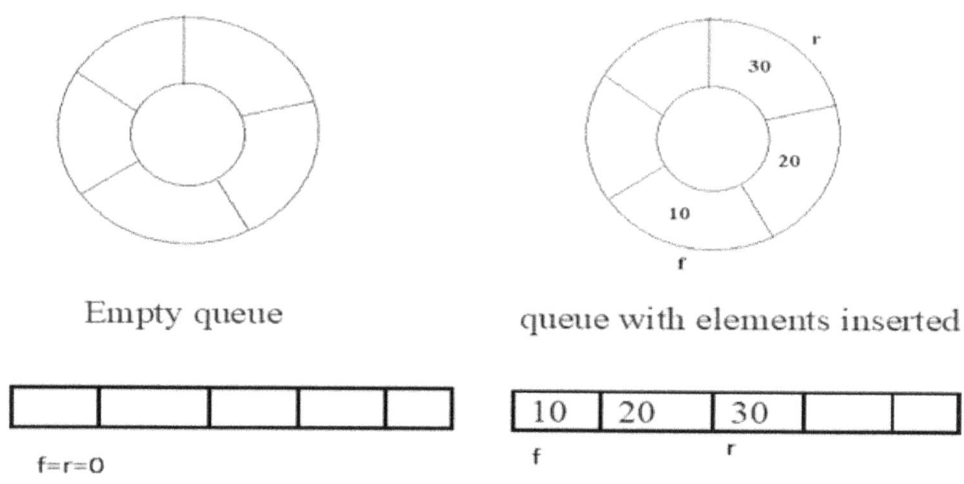

Fig 5.10: Pictorial Representation of a circular queue

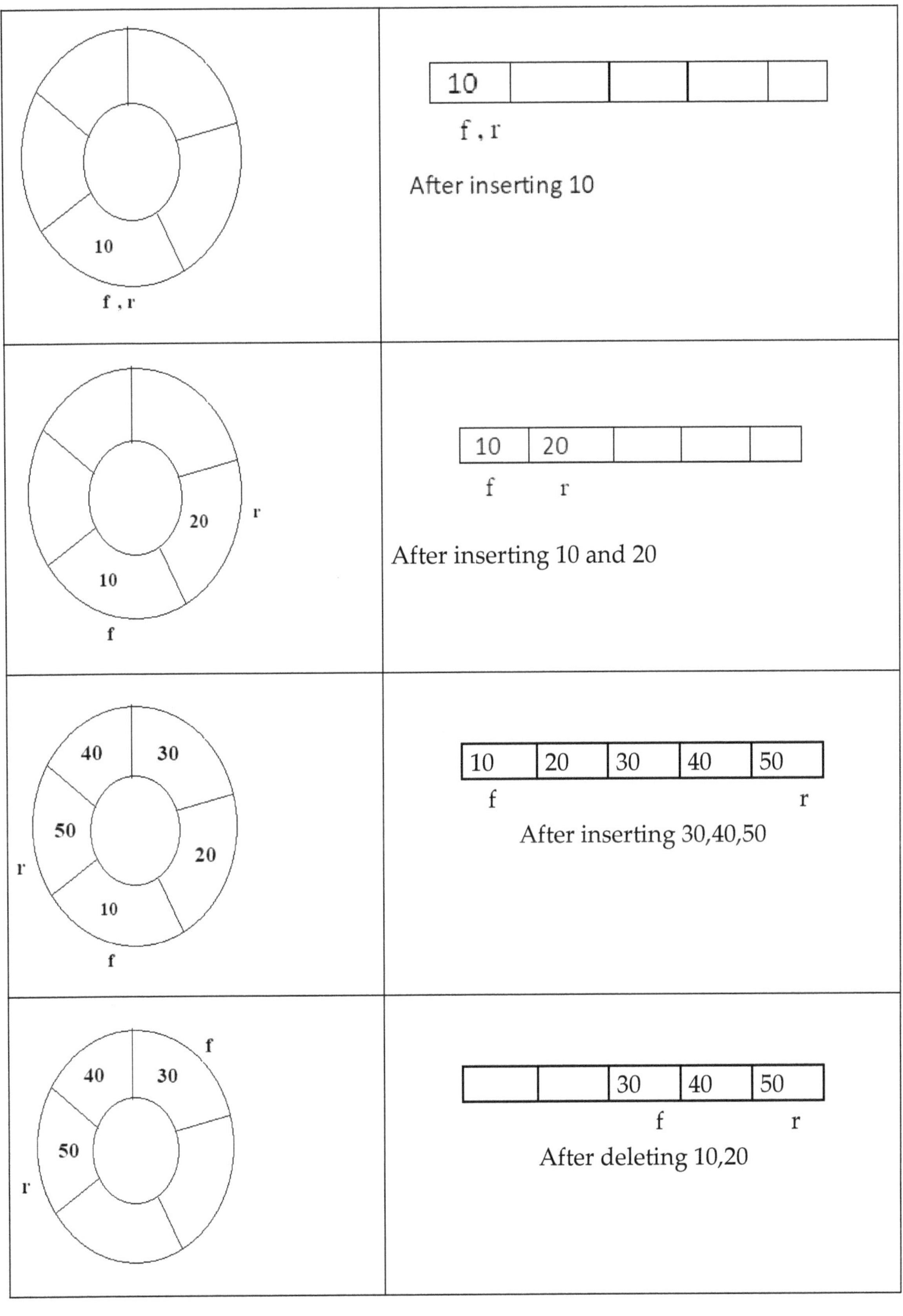

10
f , r
After inserting 10
f , r
10 20
f r
After inserting 10 and 20
10 20 30 40 50
f r
After inserting 30,40,50
30 40 50
f r
After deleting 10,20

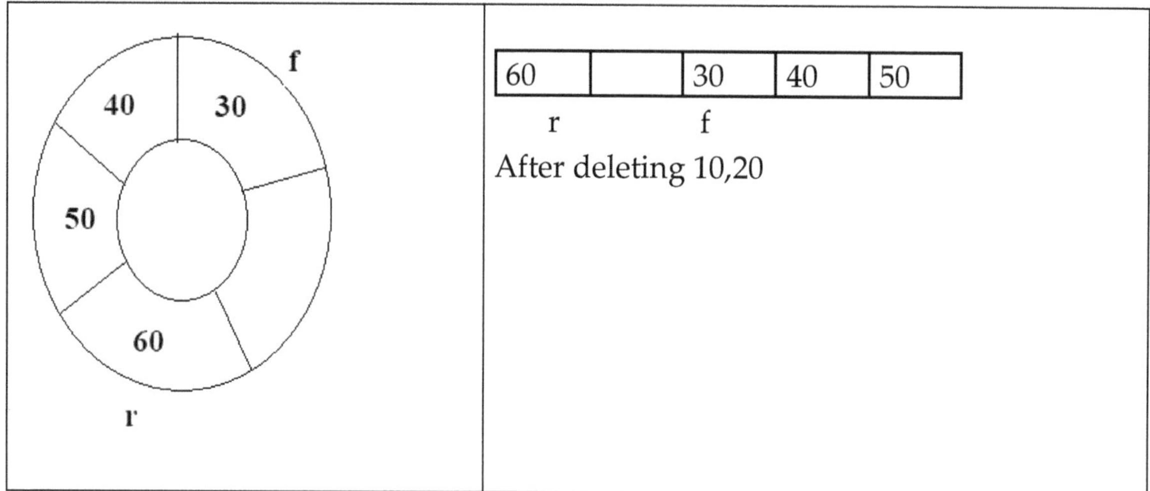

Fig 5.11: Pictorial Representation of a circular queue

5.19   Other operations on Stack

IsEmpty():

The IsEmpty() function will check whether the stack is empty or not. The function returns a Boolean value. If the stack is empty, it returns a non-zero value and if the stack is not empty it returns a zero value.

```
int IsEmpty()
{
if(top==-1)
        return 1;
    else
        return 0;
}
```

IsFull():

The IsFull() function will check whether the stack is full or not. The function returns a Boolean value. If the stack is full, it returns a non-zero value and if the stack is not full it returns a zero value.

```
int IsFull()
{
if(top==STACK_SIZE-1)
        return 1;
    else
        return 0;
}
peek():
```

```
The peek() function returns the top most element of stack.
int peek()
{
if(top==-1)
{
            printf("Stack empty\n");
            return 0;
    }
    else
            return s[top];
}
```

5.20   Exercises

Stack

1. Check for balanced parentheses in an expression
2. Reverse a Stack using queue
3. Delete Middle element from stack
4. Reverse individual words
5. How to implement a queue using two stacks?
6. Implement Stack using Queues
7. Implement a stack using a single queue
8. Evaluate Postfix Expression
9. Sort a stack using a temporary stack.
10. Reverse a stack using recursion
11. Infix to Postfix Conversion using Stack
12. Implement two stacks in an array
13. Length of the longest valid substring
14. Find index of closing bracket for a given opening bracket in an expression
15. Next Greater Frequency Element
16. Check if two expressions with brackets are same

Queues

17. Implement a Deque
18. Implement a Circular Queue
19. Implement Stack using Queues
20. Implement Queue using Two Stacks
21. Implement a Queue using a Stack
22. Reverse a queue using recursion
23. Implement Priority Queue using Linked List